THE
GIANTS
IN MY MIDST

MASOOD ABDUL-HAQQ

To Ma'isah, Ahmad and Sufyan.

May you reach the stars from my shoulders.

TABLE OF CONTENTS

Introduction

I am a Black American Muslim man.

These four identities carry separate responsibilities, sources of pride, and stigmas. Together, they make people like me stand out no matter where we go, for better or worse. In America, being Black with a non-Christian faith, Black with an Arabic name, American with Black skin, or Muslim with an American dialect have plenty in common. They all tend to make one exotic enough for the majority to be intrigued by but strange enough to be kept at arm's length, if not outright hated.

But we are the sons and daughters of rebels who changed their names and recalibrated their faith in their twenties. Like them, we don't accept the status quo. Also, like them, we are grappling with what it means to be a productive person of faith within the fabric of an increasingly complicated society.

Who am I? My pursuit of the answer to this question has taken me through public schools, private schools, boarding schools, alternative schools, open campuses, Community Colleges, and for-profit colleges before finally graduating from a University. Today I find myself in leadership positions in the business, health, and nonprofit sectors. In addition, I often travel and enjoy a robust family life.

But nothing prepared me for who and what I am today, like my experiences with specific individuals I call the Giants in my Midst.

In this book, I share my struggles with procrastination and finding passion as an adolescent and young adult. I call the people who helped me through them, Giants, because, by the Creator's grace, they lifted me from a low place and inspired me to get on a path toward higher ground. To quote the late philosopher Ermias Asghedom, the highest human act is to inspire.

Too often, we reserve our best compliments for eulogies. This book is about giving deserving people flowers while they can still smell them.

This book is about how I used the people around me to ignite passion and chart a path to success. It's about the Giants who helped transform my mindset into that of a productive member of society.

This book is for the impoverished dreamer, the chronically bored, the indifferent, the unimpressed, the indecisive, the gifted, and the talented. I was, and in many ways still am, all those things.

I broke the Giants into three sections: the Foundational, the Reformative, and the Inspirational. Then, after introducing you to them using key stories, I extract the principles I learned from these Giants during my climb from impoverished at-risk youth to the family man, community leader, business owner, and motivational speaker I am today.

In a century similar to how we react to the Renaissance ages, people will be astonished to learn we knew and interacted with each other. To prove this, in February of 2021, I decided to feature 28 people in my immediate circle whose legacies should and will last well beyond their final breath. I wrote an essay a day for 28 days and posted it on Facebook and Instagram with a photo of the featured person and the hashtag #TheGiantsInMyMidst.

The first criterion for anyone featured was that they had to be someone with whom I had at least one personal interaction and was inspired by. The second was the answer to the question:

If a world-changing event hit us and it was up to me to rebuild society, who would I want to be by my side?

After over 50,000 impressions online and a loud demand for the series to be put into book form, here we are.

I have two main goals as you enjoy this book. My first goal is for you to apply the principles taught by the Giants in My Midst. My second one is that you reflect on your life, identify your giants, and tell them thank you.

PART I:
The Foundation

Both nature and nurture influence us as we develop our purpose.

To know why the Giants in My Midst and the principles they taught me are essential, you must first understand where I came from. The Foundational Giants are the people from whom I learned my core values and early habits. Mostly from love, but some through traumatic experiences. So, naturally, this group begins with my parents, who, through their means, efforts and decisions, determined my earliest experiences and taught me who they wanted me to be.

I learned about my labels and how society perceived them during this time.

Both nature and nurture are influenced by trauma and reproduce it. Trauma can be passed down through family genes and tradition just as quickly as learned through events experienced with peers. Yet, in the Black American community, trauma is often treated as taboo, worn as a badge of honor, or made light of. Rarely is it addressed or treated.

My father was a soft-spoken, mild-mannered version of himself by the time I came around, thanks to his love and appreciation for the Prophet Muhammad. My maternal grandfather was a polished, well-respected, history-making orthodontist featured in magazines. So why could I get so angry at losses or perceived slights that my chest would swell with hot air, my eyes would fill with water, and my ears would burn? Why did I escalate dangerous situations to the point of chaos?

My father did not share his exploits as a wild young man on the streets of Indianapolis until well after I'd had my own in the streets of Atlanta. Likewise, my mother didn't reveal how her father's temper nearly destroyed her family while he was putting himself through school. So I was deprived of critical lessons from my father and maternal grandfather because the trauma that came with those lessons remained unprocessed and unshared. As a result, I didn't understand the hot-tempered, daredevil streaks that came naturally to me. But more importantly, I was not equipped to handle them.

To advance as individuals or as a group, we must be thoroughly transparent about where we come from and what we have been through. Then we can learn from our mistakes, shore up our deficiencies and build on our strengths in shorter cycles.

Islam

I have always loved the camaraderie and sense of duty to serve that Islam promotes. The idea of this vast, calculated, and beautiful creation having one phenomenal, powerful-beyond-comprehension creator makes much more sense to me than random elements simply combusting and evolving. By age six, I could ask the next logical question about that theory - "Where did those elements come from?"

Don't get me wrong; everything in the universe constantly evolves. I wouldn't be alive to write this book if not for that fact. However, the Supreme Being who created it first is also in control of its evolution. I wouldn't be surprised if Adam and Eve were simply the first homo sapiens and if all other human forms we have discovered were different species altogether.

For as long as I can remember, life has felt too much like a high-stakes game for me to believe death is the end. Of course, any high-stakes game must have winners and losers. But it must also have rules.

There are too many examples of beauty and mercy in this world for me to believe the Creator hates us or wants us to fail. So the idea of the Creator sending us guides in the form of written instructions (Torah, Bible, Qur'an, etc.) and model humans (Moses, Jesus, Muhammad, etc.) has always made sense to me. Similarly, I could never make sense of the "Say I'm with him for total salvation" narrative. We are accountable for our actions if this world shows us nothing else.

But like many second-generation Muslims, the heightened expectation of religious scholarship without a roadmap to success in this life did not sit well with me. I just wanted to be a regular Muslim who prays, fasts in Ramadan, gives charity and smiles. But I wanted to do it without the pressure of memorizing and retaining the entire Qur'an or adopting customs from countries I'd never been to. And I certainly didn't want to be poor due to hating or fearing this life, its challenges, and its bounties.

You'll read in this section how the lifestyle I was being pushed toward conflicted with what I was facing every day and led me to rebellion. My approach to parenting was born during this period of my life. Because of my childhood experiences, I realize that hiding who I am to protect my children is oxymoronic. No one can know better what my child is going through in a tense or challenging situation than the father whose blood runs in their veins.

Fortunately, the beauty of community is the variety of adult examples available to a misfit child. In this section, in addition to my parents, I highlight two entrepreneurs who offered a glimpse at the balance I sought. I gravitated toward men with excellent communication skills who were masters of a craft and women who were nurturing but stern. I also include some of my earliest friends who taught me how to navigate and survive the hood.

Chapter 1: Me

Abiquiu

I spent my formative years in the Dar-al Islam community in Abiquiu, New Mexico — home to locals who called themselves Chicanos and a peaceful group of Muslims of European, Arab, Hispanic and Jewish descent. We lived a modest life, moving three times in seven years within the small mountain town. But as a child, I never felt poor. Life in Abiquiu meant having rivers to cross, forests of trees to climb and pick fruit from, fields to run, mountains to hike, and friends to tag along. Nothing about that made me feel poor.

Me vs. the Field

"Papa, don't preach. I'm in trouble deep…"

My older sister Kaleema, a pre-teen enjoying a perfect cocktail of freedom, time, and space, led her four younger siblings on a trek through the bosque. The cool, crisp morning showed signs of giving way to a glorious summer afternoon. As was our custom, we trailed Kaleema in our birth order, putting me second to last in line. Defiantly singing Madonna's latest hit, Kaleema led us in figure eights around large cottonwood trees and weeping willows, through creeks, and over ditches.

"You know you're not supposed to be singing that song!" My sister Sumayyah was four years Kaleema's junior but was by far the most responsible of our mother's crew. Kaleema looked back, smirking at her annoyed little sister, and turned up the volume. "CAUSE I'VE MADE UP MY MIIIIND, I'M KEEPIN MY BAYBAY!"

She skipped diagonally toward the edge of the bosque and stopped to admire the scene while we caught up. My older brother Yaseen, younger sister Najwa, and I gleefully traced Kaleema's steps, repeating after our fearless leader, "I'm gonna keep my baybay!" in chorus as we made our way out of the bosque and back to Abu's worksite.

Once out of the bosque, the bright New Mexico sun beamed directly into my eyes, adding a sense of euphoria to our adventure as we approached the majestic green two-acre field. The house my father was helping build sat atop a foothill on the other side of the field.

Suddenly, Kaleema took off in a sprint. We raced to keep up, dodging holes dug by prairie dogs and tall grass that could slow us down and hide snakes. This sort of sprint was an everyday thing for us, so I nimbly dodged the field's pitfalls and focused on two things: beating Yaseen and not letting Najwa beat me.

Because of the sharecropper Moore blood in our veins and the fact that we hiked a mile each way to get to our nearest friends' houses every day, we were all abnormally athletic and strong relative to our peers. About 12 months apart, we were highly competitive, even though we never spoke about it. Kaleema had the most personality, so I wanted to develop an even brighter character than she had. Yaseen was the strongest and fastest, so I constantly challenged him or found physical feats that I could be better than him. Najwa was a straight-A student, so I had to get 99s or 100s on every assignment.

In my mind, winning this race across this field was realistic.

Did I care that my older and much taller sister had gotten a head start?

That I had never beaten my brother?

Hell no. This race was mine for the taking.

I lengthened my strides to catch Yaseen and looked back to make sure Najwa wasn't in a position to gain ground on me.

Wind in our faces and weeds at our shins, Yaseen and I both passed Sumayyah early and closed on Kaleema before coming to the barbed wire fence, which served as the de facto finish line.

Behind us, Najwa edged out Sumayyah by a nose.

Kaleema may have won, but given that she had me by almost seven years, seeing that gap narrow between us at the end gave me a deep satisfaction about my blossoming physical prowess.

We ducked through the barbed wire fence and headed toward the job site. Stepping around cactuses and keeping our eyes peeled for snakes, we reached the top of the hill. Despite the results of the foot race, we had fallen back into a single chronological file, with Kaleema again playing the ringleader role. By now, because of the proximity to my father, Madonna had been reduced to a faint hum.

Left to Right: Me, Yaseen, Sumayyah and Najwa

Oh... Well

Once on flat ground, there was a puddle 15 feet in front of us.

Kaleema took a few steps and hopped over the water with a foot to spare.

Sumayyah followed by sprinting and clearing it.

Yaseen took two giant, slow steps and lept clean over it, landing on the same foot from which he took off.

Not to be outdone, I walked to the edge of the puddle and came to a complete stop so I could take off with no head start and clear it.

I pushed off the ground with both feet as hard as I could.

When I reached the apex of my jump, I thrust my little legs in front of me with my hands reaching toward my toes.

My toes came down on the opposite edge of the puddle, but my heels were inside. My toes slipped off, and I was plunging into this seemingly bottomless pit.

It was an incomplete well.

Each of my senses became shocked by a stark new reality.

My siblings' silhouettes revealed panic above, but they rapidly grew smaller as their voices became more muffled and eventually muted. Everything became pitch black. A reflexive gasp for air filled my mouth with thick mud. I felt myself sinking but thought I would feel the bottom of this puddle with my foot at some point and use my super strength to jump back to the top.

But the bottom never came.

Instead, something else, either a primal instinct, an angel, or both, took over at that point.

Despite having yet to graduate past the doggy paddling portion of swim lessons at the Ghost Ranch pool, I felt myself floating back toward the surface until the silhouettes returned, and I could hear my siblings shouting and crying.

"There he is!" Najwa pointed at my mud-covered body as my back broke through the surface of the incomplete well. As I rotated my face upward to breathe again, Yaseen stared on, frozen in shock. Kaleema had run to get help, and the four of us shared a "what next?" moment that probably lasted about a second but felt like an eternity as I wiggled and splashed for my life.

Suddenly, Sumayyah reached into the well with a piece of wire she had found on the ground, which I grabbed, and she yanked me out with one pull.

I had no idea the goodie two-shoe girl I had just dusted in a race across the field had that in her. It was a real mama-lifting-a-car-to-rescue-her-baby moment.

And it saved my life.

Covered from head to toe, I wiped the mud and dead mosquitoes out of my eyes, blew them out of my nose, and began gathering information on what exactly just happened to me from my excited and traumatized siblings as they recapped the story.

I was sitting on some spread-out newspapers on the shag carpet inside Old Brown, my father's brown 1979 Ford Econoline conversion van. My mother and father were there with me, laughing at the spectacle while pointing out that they would have responded more quickly had we not been pranking them all week. My siblings kept saying they thought I was going to die or that I was dead.

This could've been the saddest obituary photo ever.

At age six, I didn't have a firm grasp on the concept of death yet, but I was rapidly developing one. From what my siblings described, I knew death was at the bottom of that well. And I knew that I had beaten it with Sumayyah and someone or something else's help. But I was also becoming quite resolute on something else:

I was alive for a reason.

That, and I don't mess with water.

Goldfish to Pirhana

When my family and I moved to the West End of Atlanta, Georgia in the Fall of 1991 — just as the city bustled to ready itself for the 1996 Olympics, it became harder to ignore what we lacked.

Abu was reluctant to make a move — his first choice was Detroit. The move to Atlanta was all about Umi finding herself, finishing her degree at an HBCU, and introducing her sheltered kufi and khimar wearing Chicano dialect having children to what it meant to be Black in America.

She knew we needed to meet our tribe.

These factors ultimately outweighed the reality that either way, Detroit or Atlanta, we were moving to a place where drugs, robbery, and murder were a fact of life, where the likelihood of going to prison was more significant than the likelihood of going to college. Where the people meant to guide and protect us instead see a young Black man with potential as a threat or an unrealistic dreamer. Where I would learn they couldn't chase me if I didn't run.

I was a goldfish dumped into a tank full of piranhas, and I'd have to learn how to pretend to be a piranha if I wanted to survive.

Potential & Procrastination

If I was going to survive the move, I had a steep learning curve. First, I had to get beyond the social culture shock of moving from a fairytale world to a big city and figure out who I would become. Second, I had to be bold enough to continue to take leaps of faith without fear of drowning.

While many of my friends had artistic or athletic talents, most of mine had to do with my brain.

My father often tells a story, incredulously, about me carefully studying my hand as I opened and closed a fist in a flowing succession from index finger to pinky and back, only minutes after being born. To him, this was an indication of immense intellectual capacity.

I couldn't draw, swim or hit a backflip if my life depended on it. But somehow, by second grade, I could recall, with vivid detail, almost anything I had laid eyes on at any point in time and calculate complex math problems in my head.

Adults were either entertained or intimidated by my abilities to do things they couldn't. It got to a point where it was easier to appease them with flashes of brilliance than to put in the work needed to accomplish long-term goals.

Before long, I learned how to manipulate adults with these talents.

Not because I got a kick out of being manipulative or defiant, but because I lacked ambition or a sense of direction, and flashes of brilliance made adults leave me alone about the future. Don't get me wrong, the adults in my life did a great job of instilling in my mind that the world was my oyster and I could do whatever I wanted. But they would then turn around and devote their time and efforts to other children whose futures I could only deduce were less bright than mine.

"That's just Masood. He's gonna be fine" was a common refrain.

"The squeaky wheel gets the oil" was another explanation for why kids who achieved less than me got more attention and more incentives to excel.

As a result, I grew up with a sense that I was special — and entitled to success. Through this lens, I developed an attitude of "why dedicate myself to one thing when I can do anything?" But unfortunately, since all I needed to do to be considered exceptional was show up, I did not develop a consistently strong work ethic or sense of urgency.

14

The stories and lessons in the books I read always depicted the road to success as a narrow, winding one littered with potholes and pitfalls. But nothing I was accomplishing as a young student felt the least difficult to obtain. So even as the plaques, ribbons, and straight-A report cards piled up, I wasn't sure I was as remarkable as everyone seemed to think.

> The constant praise and accolades inflated my ego, but once I was alone, I would feel a crippling imposter syndrome.

I still needed to learn how to apply my gifts to the real world.

The Hero's Journey

The main characters in my favorite books and films were pulled toward their destinies.

For example, Encyclopedia Brown was a prodigious kid with a burning desire to be a detective. He was passionate about figuring out who wronged his client, and he would stop at nothing until he did just that.

In Where the Red Fern Grows, Billy Coleman wasn't brilliant, but his passion for hunting raccoons led him to perform backbreaking labor for two years, then walk barefoot for miles to buy Old Dan and Little Anne, his hunting dogs. The three won competitions and enough money to change Billy's family's life forever.

In the Never Ending Story, Atreyu braves a mutant wolf, horse engulfing swamps, and turtle snot storms to save himself, an Empress, and ostensibly, the world from a mysterious force called The Nothing.

I couldn't relate.

These works of art informed me of one thing:

Passion, not intellect,
is the common denominator for
truly successful people.

And I wanted some.

I was most comfortable alone. I still am to this day. But back then, I loved being alone, doing things with no real purpose or benefit. The Nothing, if you will. Though I could look the part of a diligent worker or world saver for a few hours at a time, I was no match for The Nothing when no one was watching.

Year after year, I watched as my peers declared their passions and began to pursue them. But intellect and arrogance often go hand-in-hand. So no matter how smart I was or how many accomplishments I accumulated, nothing compelled me to choose a direction.

Instead, I showed up, performed at an above-average level with minimal effort, and retreated to The Nothing. As a result of this pattern, I became a master procrastinator, paralyzed by the spectacle unfolding all around me.

Still.

One of my business mentors, Lamar Tyler, calls me a paralyzed perfectionist.

The proceeding helped me press play on my life story.

GIANT PRINCIPLE:

Take the Leap, like 6-year-old me, over the well. But not before knowing what you're getting yourself into.

Chapter 2:
Abu

Sulaiman Abdul-Haqq
Teacher, Servant of the Truth

"Peace is with those who
follow the guidance."

The opening of Abu's voicemail greeting hasn't changed in twenty-plus years. It is very telling because he has lived his entire life searching for peace. He's done it following the guidance that saved him.

One calm night in Itta Bena, Mississippi, in 1951, W.B. and Zirlee Moore smuggled their two boys, Robert Lee and Larry Eugene, off of the farm that W.B. had labored on since he was a child. They looked back longingly at the town that bore him and set out to lay roots in the promised land of Indianapolis, Indiana.

I'm not sure what else to call a farm in Jim Crow Mississippi that a black worker had to escape from other than a slave plantation. Some would say that made the Moore family runaway slaves. I say it made them followers of guidance seeking peace.

Larry Moore is Abu, which means 'my father' in Arabic. Abu is the only thing I've ever called my dad to his face. So it would be weird for me to use anything else here.

What's In a Name?

Abu experienced several more near-death encounters growing up in Indianapolis. He built a reputation in his neighborhood as "Lil Mo," the short, stocky guy with an even shorter fuse and a propensity to go toward danger in the streets. It was a risky lifestyle, to be sure. But from 1940 until 1973, the United States military drafted young men between the ages of 19 and 37 to fill vacancies. So to a young man during those times, nothing was more dangerous than the Vietnam draft.

By 1968, Abu was a radical young man who rejected his given name, replacing it with Hodari Maskini or "Brave Poor." When the dreaded "Uncle Sam Wants You" letter came to Abu, he proved the Brave part of his chosen name by picking his 'fro out, dressing up in a dashiki, and screaming to the recruiters about how badly he wanted to kill. Sure enough, he got his wish; the Army found him unfit to serve.

Having just put an enormous target on his back for the feds to see, Abu decided to leave Indianapolis for New York in search of peace.

In search of the truth.

Abu shared an apartment in New York with his mentor, who converted to Islam and took the name Muhammad Abdul-Haqq. After failing to latch on to the teachings of Noble Drew Ali, the Black Hebrew Israelites, and several other emerging religious and philosophical groups, Abu took his shahadah a few weeks later, converting to Islam. His teacher Khalid Yaseen gave him the name Sulaiman. Abu had a long-standing fascination with King Solomon, the wealthiest of all kings who could speak the language of the animals, so he happily accepted the Arabic version of the great prophet's name as his own.

Thinking Muhammad was Abu's blood brother, the other men in the group added Abdul-Haqq to Sulaiman, and Abu didn't mind because Al-Haqq means The Truth. It's one of the most potent of the 99 known attributes of God, so a Muslim can only be 'Abd, or slave, of Al-Haqq. That's how Larry Eugene Moore became Sulaiman Abdul-Haqq. It's also the origin story of why people look at my name and ask,

"No, like, where are you FROM from?"

After studying Islam in New York for several years, Abu's teachers sent him back home to Indianapolis to spread Islam there. Once back home, he would play his flute in the park and tell people who would approach him about the beautiful religion that transformed a once-feared brute into what they saw. Over time, a group formed around Abu. The Masjid that this group established was the first in the city, if not the entire state. It is called Masjid Al-Fajr and still thrives to this day.

Abu didn't stay in 'Nap' long, though. After a brief stop in Tennessee, where he got married twice, the second time to my mother, he moved his new young bride to Fort Worth, Texas, in 1978. The couple each had young daughters but wasted no time having more. They added additions in October 1979, November 1980, December 1981, and July 1983. We lived in a small house and then an unairconditioned one-bedroom apartment. Abu worked hard and would be gone all day, but his income was simply no match for a wife and five kids.

The Dar al-Islam Hustle

When Abu got word about a long-term building project funded by a Saudi princess in a beautiful, secluded town where the cost of living was cheap, his ears perked up. The promise of private Islamic education for us pushed him over the top. Before we knew it, we packed everything we owned, and Fort Worth was in our rearview mirror.

After the Princess found out a group of Sufis called Naqshbandis led Dar Al-Islam, she stopped sending them money, and construction on the Masjid and Madressa stopped.

These Saudis did capitalism, sexism, and racism, but by no means did they do Sufism.

That's me and Yaseen sitting on Abu's lap on the bottom left.

Left to right top: Yaseen, Umi, Abu, Me
Bottom: Sumayyah, Najwa, Kaleema

After the Dar-al Islam job ended, most of Abu's workdays were not as eventful or memorable as when he almost lost me to the well. Abiquiu had a population of fewer than 300 people and thus fewer homes to build or improve. So Abu would usually travel to Santa Fe with his coworker, a stocky, red-bearded Iowan named Abdur-Rahim Lutz, in a small Datsun truck to build or improve houses belonging to very wealthy people. A skilled wood craftsman and self-titled "Carpentaire Extraordinaire," Abu could have made a killing in America's hottest second-home market.

Thanks to its secluded natural landscape, rich culture, and sparse population, Santa Fe attracted a who's who of the rich and famous, including Oprah Winfrey, Ted Danson, and Jim Henson. And while their neighbors may not have been as recognizable, plenty of them were just as rich.

Abu could have charged a premium on his custom-carved wood cabinets and shelves, but negotiation was not his strong suit. So often, he would accept the first offer, flagrantly underbidding the market, and spend months on projects that only paid something once completed. And when he did get paid, it was still just a fraction of what his mastery was worth. This pattern forced my mother to be creative in feeding and clothing us. Abu's rationale was rooted in the Islamic belief in Qadr, defined in English as Divine Decree. He would often preach to us that "Allah knows exactly how many breaths you will take, grains of rice you will eat, and dollars you will make. There is nothing anyone can do to change that!"

Allah decreed that Umi would grow unsatisfied with life in Abiquiu.

Hijratul Ghetto

In September 1991, my family packed everything we owned into Old Brown, Umi's 1987 blue Jeep Grand Cherokee, and a small U-Haul trailer. Yaseen and I rode in Old Brown with Abu, while Sumayyah and Najwa rode in the Jeep with Umi.

We covered over 1,400 miles. The route took us through scenic northern New Mexico mountainsides and endless stretches of flatlands. We held our noses through Texas cow farm towns and stopped to rest and refuel in Oklahoma City before being hypnotized by the rhythmic bumpiness of the aging Arkansas highways.

But the clearest memories of my first significant migration begin with an unplanned pit stop in the seediest part of West Memphis, Arkansas, that Old Brown could find to break down in. After a heated discussion between Umi and Abu, the girls kept moving down the future I-22 corridor toward Birmingham and Atlanta.

Abu found a mechanic near the exit who could do the job in six hours and, presumably, based on his appearance and resources, for cheap. Yaseen was into engines and cars, so he and Abu were very much a part of the fixing process.

I was in my own world.

Sprawled out on Old Brown's shag-carpeted floor with the french doors wide open, I took inventory of my life.

I was a country boy from New Mexico who had grown up in the mountains with the children of hippies and Chicanos. I was good at chopping wood, setting fire to anything that would burn, and shooting prairie dogs. And I counted treasure hunting at the county dump among my favorite pastimes.

My introduction to Black culture was when a blonde-haired, blue-eyed teenager from Spain named Yasin Cabre gave my brother and me a ride in his truck while bumping *The Ghetto* by Too $hort and *My Mind is Playing Tricks on Me* by The Geto Boys.

I loved how funky *The Ghetto* was. The bass line reminded me of one of my dad's Isaac Hayes or Stevie Wonder records. But the lyrics were haunting me.

In the song, Too $hort raps about slangin' dope, how to survive, and asks questions like "will he kill … before he dies?"

My Mind is Playing Tricks on Me was no better.

As the sun set, the proximity to the freeway made it so each passing car felt like a noisy reminder of the progress we were not making. I hopped out of the van and walked around to the front, where the three grease monkeys were. Hands in my pockets and rocking back and forth, I asked;

"Abu?"

"Yes, son?"

"Are we moving to the Ghetto?"

Abu paused and averted his eyes.

"Get back in the van, boy. And crank the engine."

Sitting in the driver's seat was usually reserved for Yaseen, but he was under the hood. So I hurried up, climbed into the seat, and made my best impression of Abu when he cranked Old Brown up. Turning the key with my left foot on the brake while vigorously pumping the gas with my right, I muttered to myself, "c'mon, c'mon, c'mon…"

The engine roared to life with a bit of coaxing, and I could feel it vibrating under the carpeted engine cover next to my right knee. The grease monkeys let out a cheer, and I imagined it was for me.

In a bit of time, we were back on the road. Atlanta was on the horizon, and I couldn't get over the fact that Abu had ignored my question.

We were moving to the ghetto.

I was sure of it.

No matter how many Kriss Kross songs I had listened to or articles on urban slang I read in Sumayyah's Seventeen magazine, I just knew I wasn't ready for the ghetto. Thanks to Seventeen magazine,

THE GIANTS IN MY MIDST

though, I was pretty confident that in the ghetto, they would call Old Brown a "hooptie."

West End Place

Late September in Atlanta is a sight to behold.

Unlike the suffocatingly humid July and August parts of summer, late September is the good stuff. The sun beams from far enough away that you can gaze at the perfect blue sky without shielding your eyes.

The temperatures are typically in the 80s, with a cool, sweat-activating breeze swooping in from time to time to cool you down. Kids can play as long as the sun is out; luckily, it is for 12 hours in Atlanta in September. The towering oak, maple, and cedar trees have no pattern because they were there well before the buildings. But when seeing them for the first time, they pop against that majestic sky in a way that makes 5k blush. To top it all off, the shade that they provide feels complete. No sun peaks through, and the temperature in that shade feels 20 degrees cooler.

This scene was the backdrop as Abu pushed the blue Jeep carrying our family down West End Place.

DJ Jazzy Jeff and The Fresh Prince had scored a worldwide hit the previous summer called Summertime. The scene that unfolded before us as we drove down West End Place could have very well been the subject of the fourth verse of that song. A Muslim remix version because while the weather was hot, these girls were not dressing less. These Black girls, in loose-fitting American clothes and colorful khimars, played rhythmic clapping games, hopscotch, and double-dutch on the sidewalks. Black boys in kufis that had their names crocheted into the side chased and slap boxed each other.

I'm not sure what the speed limit was on West End Place; it felt like Abu was driving two miles an hour. So everybody saw us.

When their eyes made it to me, they saw my hands pressed against the window and my eyes and jaw wide open.

It was love at first sight.

Remember, we were coming from New Mexico - seeing Black people was worthy of being remembered and discussed for weeks. During these encounters, usually in Santa Fe or Albuquerque, pointing at and making a beeline to the other black people was customary. The general question for both parties: "What in the world are you doing here?"

The second I laid eyes on West End Place, I knew we wouldn't be having those encounters anytime soon. We belonged here, I thought, as Abu pulled the Cherokee over, and all six of us got out.

Abu spotted the words "West End Community Mosque" on the front of a small cream-colored house with forest green trim and instinctively began his way toward it.

We had already made Dhuhr — the second of our five daily prayers — before our late check out at the Days Inn. But, Asr, the late afternoon prayer was not in yet. So Yaseen and I glanced at each other, silently communicating; what *salat is this dude making now?*

We could hear shouts, laughter, and basketballs from West End Park just ahead. Then, finally, Yaseen spoke up and asked, "Abu, can we go to the park?"

I started leaning and taking a step toward the park to help Abu decide. Abu glanced at a tall, lanky man in overalls, glasses, and a kufi on the corner who was monitoring the goings-on down below and said, "Go ahead. But make sure you stick together."

Yaseen and I excitedly made our way down the sidewalk past the tall man who looked at us as if he was adding two new faces to his mental monitoring database.

"As Salaamu Alaikum!" we said to the man in unison. It is customary for an arriving party to give the greetings first.

"Wa Alaikum salaam," the man replied in a deep, slow drawl without breaking his gaze. "Who is your father?" the man asked.

Yaseen and I turned around and pointed at the bearded and turbaned man following the guidance into the Masjid. The tall man nodded and stepped aside as if to dismiss us. (Chapter 4's The Shed begins here).

The Historic West End

Atlanta was never Abu's idea.

When leaving Abiquiu became inevitable, his preference was to move to Detroit. Blue-collar rust belt towns with five-month-long winters brought back warm memories to the Indianapolis native. In addition, Detroit was home to two prominent Black Muslim scholars and a well-respected Imam. But Detroit had two other factors that probably appealed to Abu. First, Detroit was a blue-collar city where a hard-working carpenter of modest means, such as Abu, would be appreciated.

On the other hand, Atlanta was Black Hollywood long before Tyler Perry bought the former Confederate Army fort McPherson and turned it into a sprawling production studio. Moreover, the existence of Spelman, Morehouse, Morris Brown colleges, and Clark Atlanta University — collectively known as the Atlanta University Center or the AUC — ensured a new wave of thousands of bright young Black men and women would call Georgia's capital city home each year. So by 1991, Atlanta was more of a boule city, where Black elites had been in power for decades, going back to the Civil Rights era and subsequent election of Maynard Jackson as mayor in 1973.

In Atlanta, there was an expectation of ambition. An expectation of *more*.

The crown jewels of the AUC are Morehouse, a private college for Black men, and Spelman, a private college for Black women. Some notable graduates of Morehouse and Spelman were Dr. Martin Luther King, his mother Alberta and daughter Bernice, Samuel L. Jackson, Spike Lee, and, more recently, Stacey Abrams.

Whether to attend an AUC school, Georgia State University, Agnes Scott College, Georgia Tech, or Emory, once Black students from around the country taste Atlanta's rich and diverse Black culture, they often stay long after graduation. Many come from cities and towns across America, which do not allow them to explore or appreciate Black culture the way Atlanta does, and they view a return to those places as a digression. Well-off and wealthy Black residents of Atlanta even have an unofficial section on the Southwest side of town called Cascade. Similar status symbol enclaves have since developed throughout the city today. But in the 1990s, the dream of buying a home in Cascade inspired the most ambitious young Black professionals.

For those who preferred to ignore the less fortunate side of being Black in America, the West End sat, rather inconveniently, between the AUC and Cascade. So its drug, prostitution, violence, and HIV problems were a cautionary tale as they rolled through it to get from elite private college education to the privilege of upper-middle-class living.

But the West End was not all crime and poverty. It was also the heart of Afrocentric Atlanta. Soul Food and Caribbean restaurants, organic health food, and Black literature stores thrived on Ralph David Abernathy Boulevard. Ralph David, as we called it, extended from the

Mall West End to Beecher Street, where it turned into Cascade Road. So if you wanted to buy homemade black soap, incense, oils, a plate of neckbones, oxtails, or yams, clothing items made from kente cloth, or catch a performance from an African dance troop, the West End was the place for you.

The West End was not the place for Abu.

Tablighi Jamat

Abu had tried most Afrocentric groups during his explorative phase in New York before becoming Muslim. A staunch believer in the concept of Tawheed, or the absolute oneness of God, he didn't like those groups' tendency to call themselves Gods or god-like. So after settling on Islam, he gravitated toward a sect formed by Pakistanis and focused on missionary-style efforts aimed at Muslims, called the Tablighi Jamat. Tablighis pointed to the fact that the Prophet Muhammad's companions died all over the world as proof that being a Da'ee – a person who actively spreads Islam – was the ultimate calling of a true Muslim. The Tablighi Jamaat used select texts to devise a system that prescribed how many days a Da'ee should strive to be "on the path of Allah," which was anywhere but home, with the right intentions.

To emulate the estimated length of time the Sahabahs spent in the path, Tablighis are encouraged to go out in Jamaat, or groups, to other cities for three, ten, 40, or 120 days. While in these cities, they sleep in the Masjid and do helpful things called khitma before performing something called Jola in the late afternoon. Jola is when the jamaat recruits a guide from the community who can show them where other Muslims live, go to those people's houses unannounced, and try to convince the man of the house to come to the masjid for a short talk after Maghrib. I've suffered second-hand embarrassment for many Brothers that we ambushed during Jola as they stuffed junk in closets, lit incense to mask the smell of weed smoke, or tried to explain to the woman in the house why she needed to put more clothes on for the first time.

In the talk, they try to convince the brothers to leave their jobs and families for the path of Allah.

Abu is a so-called "old worker" who is often the Jamaat's Amir or appointed leader.

One of my earliest memories is getting my first Band-Aid on my right thumb after falling off the front steps of a Masjid in Houston.

"Alhamdulillah (praise be to God)," Abu said, beaming. "There is nothing more beloved to Allah than the drop of blood shed in the Path of Allah!"

I still have the scar 37+ years later.

Later, Abu would smuggle Yaseen and me into Canada to get to a Tablighi conference known as an Ijtemah. We hid under a blanket in the back of a van while Abu charmed the border agent with his one gold toothed-smile.

Tablighi life can be wild.

The wildest thing was watching how deeply Black American men like Abu immersed themselves in the aesthetics of Tablighi culture. On pit stops between one city to the next, they would emerge from vans and flood rural rest stop bathrooms dressed in lungis and shalwar kameez like the Pakistani men who started the Tablighi Jamaat.

To purify themselves for prayer, they would remove their Arab turbans and splash water all over the sinks while cleaning their teeth with small tree branches called mishwaks and drenching their orange henna-dyed beards. Their exposed foot would be in the sink if they didn't have leather socks. If you watched and listened closely enough when they spoke, you could see them adopting the foreigners' mannerisms. Bobbing their heads side to side to agree with something or saying "…ehh how you say…" when they were searching for words as if English wasn't their first, second and third language.

I loved being Black. I loved getting picked first for every pickup basketball game because I looked the most like Michael Jordan on the playground. I loved people being afraid to fight me because of how Mike Tyson was dropping dudes. Even though I couldn't dance, I loved watching my people express themselves through rhythm and movement – how every other culture struggled hard to learn the trends we set. Being Black was so lit. And I couldn't figure out why Abu did not feel the same way.

Daddy issues are the root of all issues. I don't have much in common with Abu, but I'm grateful my issues with him are just social differences. We bond these days by strategizing how I should navigate the politics I face in my various leadership roles. He has even learned to express that he's proud of me.

I'll take it.

Sulaiman Abdul-Haqq is a Giant in My Midst.
He taught me resourcefulness.
He taught me the power of faith.
He taught me humility.

GIANT PRINCIPLE:

Seek Truth, like Abu leaving Indianapolis for New York. Peace is with those who follow their hearts.

Chapter 3:
Umi

Caught Slippin

Noticing I had not yet eaten breakfast, Umi (Arabic for my mother) handed me a banana after I finished putting my shoes on. I looked at the banana and then back at her. I preferred any fruit to the one she had just given me. I hated bananas' mushy, slimy texture, their smell, the way they didn't belong to a fruit gang like citrus, pome, or melon, the way my favorite cartoon characters slipped on the peels, everything.

And Umi knew this.

But I took it anyway and ran out the door to catch my siblings on their way to the Abiquiu Elementary school bus stop as Umi watched us go.

It wasn't my bus. Umi had decided Mr. Miguel, Abiquiu's 4th-grade teacher, would not get another chance to terrorize one of her sons after he gave Yaseen a hard time the previous year. But I still liked the walk from our mobile farmhouse to CR 155, the dirt road where the Abiquiu school bus picked my siblings up. I continued the tradition of walking with them every morning, so I could see them off and wave to my friends from my 2nd and 3rd-grade years.

I jogged to catch up with Najwa, and we rounded the corner of one of the two barns in front of our house, out of Umi's sight.

"Want a banana?" I asked Najwa, trying to hand it to her, half-peeled.

"Umm, NO. Why did you open it when you know you don't like bananas, dummy?"

I sucked my teeth and said, "Man... Umi made me take it."

Looking over my shoulder to ensure Umi couldn't see me from the kitchen window, I tossed the open banana into the shrubbery. After pausing to watch Najwa's reaction, I shared a mischievous giggle with her and jogged to catch up with Sumayyah and Yaseen near the cattle-guard that separated our property from the road. When the bus pulled up, I waved at my friend Jesse, who was on the bus. Then I returned to the house, ready for my favorite part of the day - the morning drive with Umi to El Rito Elementary, where I was attending 4th grade. As one of five children, 15 minutes alone with your favorite parent was golden. Getting that to and from school twice a day was worth the anxiety of making new friends and getting used to a new school.

I returned to a disappointed-looking Umi with her hands on her hips.

"Where is that banana?" She asked knowingly.

"Oh, the banana?" I said, buying time.

"Yes, the banana I gave you before you walked out the door."

"Oh, the *banana*! I ate it." I said, fidgeting with my fingers.

"You ate the whole banana, Masood?" She asked, crouching to get eye level with me.

"Yes... I ate it fast because I don't like how bananas feel when I chew them," I muttered, thinking the truth would mask the lie.

"I don't smell any banana on your breath. Do I have to tell your father something when he gets home tonight?"

"I threw it," I whispered quickly.

"What was that?" She stood upright.

"I threw it in the bushes."

"Do you think we're rich, Masood? Go find that banana and eat it."

She watched me like a hawk as I retrieved, washed, and scarfed down my least favorite food. Then she handed me a zip-lock bag full of almonds, raisins, dried apricots, and pumpkin seeds as we pulled off in her green 1973 Ford Maverick and started our daily conversation by saying, "You never have to lie to me, Masood."

Me, Umi, and the Maverick

What's in a Name

Umi was born Kiwanis Linda Bryant on February 22, 1955. The first child born to William J. Bryant and Patricia Golden Bryant, my grandfather was only 20 years old when young Linda, as they called her, came into the world. But he did not allow the birth of his daughter to derail him from his goals. With aspirations of becoming one of, if not the first, black orthodontists in the state of Florida, Grandaddy Bill, as we call him, set out on an ambitious path. A path that included a laser-like focus on his studies, and a move to Boston, even while Grandma Pat, as we called her, had five more children.

Instead of a typical teenage social life, young Linda was the leader of the Bryant 6, thrust into a motherhood-like role to her younger siblings, Rikk, Deron, Vincent, Michael, and Kim, before ever enjoying childhood. The stiff nature of her Catholic School education didn't offer any change of pace. Like many sheltered adolescents, by the time she graduated high school, Umi was eager to find freedom. Her brief explorative phase resulted in my sister Kaleema being born just two days after Umi's 20th birthday, not unlike her father. Also, like her father, she did not allow becoming a young parent to derail her. She enrolled in Tennessee State University, where she continued to question and challenge the status quo. She met Abu there, fell in love with the simplicity of Islam, became Muslim, and took the name Tasneem Sauda. Tasneem is a fountain in paradise, and Sauda means blessed with good fortune. Soon after becoming Muslim, Umi married Abu and took his relatively new last name. I never called her anything other than Umi.

<blockquote>

Few things have a more inhibiting effect on youthful expression and exploration than motherhood.

</blockquote>

Poverty may be a close second. Fatherhood barely squeezes into the top 10. Umi had five children by the time she was 28 years old and had spent maybe two of those years figuring out who she was. But nearly 20 of them prepared her to be a great mother. So when I said nothing about my childhood made me feel poor; make no mistake, that was Umi's doing.

Food for Thought

Before Google or YouTube, Umi taught herself how to crochet blankets when it was cold, grow and harvest vegetables from her garden, make yogurt, and bake bread from scratch when we were hungry. It was essential to Umi that we be healthy, not just full. So whether we had grocery money, food stamps, or commodities, we ate healthy, balanced meals.

Our default dinner was pinto beans and rice with something green on the side during leaner times. When a Palestinian-Mexican family moved to Abiquiu, Umi learned the recipe for a chicken, rice, and vegetable dish from the lady of the house. Umi turned it into one of her specialties, narrowing the vegetable choice to cauliflower and adding her tangy homemade yogurt to cool it down when served straight out of the pot. I didn't learn the dish's official name, Maqluba, until much later. Umi always called it "upside down" because of how she dumped it on the platter out of the pot. We loved upside down nights.

Kaleema, Sumayyah, Yaseen, Najwa, and I would eat on the floor with our hands.

Umi and Abu would share a smaller plate a few feet away. The food would be on a large round metal platter on a leather mat called a dastarkhwan. I had to google the spelling; when we said it, it sounded like "dust a con." That was Abu's south Asian/Tablighi influence, though. Most Muslims call such a mat a Ma'idah – Arabic for a tablecloth, and the name of the 5th chapter of the Qur'an, where you can read about what Muslims can and cannot eat and drink.

Umi and Abu instructed us to eat what was in front of us on the platter. This led to collaborative efforts by my siblings and me to eat shapes into the food, like houses and horses. We would admire the figure for a minute before Abu would bark at us to stop playing with our food, and Umi would add, "and eat all your barakats. I want some healthy grandchildren one day!" Barakat means blessing. Technically, the plural form is barakaat, but Umi was referring to when the Prophet Muhammad said to eat all of your food because "You do not know in what portion of your food the blessing lies."

To Umi, blessings meant a long, healthy life.

And long life for everyone in her family meant she got healthy grandchildren. So "eating your barakats" meant leaving nothing to clean up behind, not even one grain of rice.

Candy was strictly off-limits except on the two Eid holidays, Eid al Fitr after Ramadan and Eid al Adha after Hajj, the annual pilgrimage to Mecca, was complete. We started fasting in Ramadan at age seven in Abu's house. So when Eid al Fitr came after a long month of watching our friends eat at lunchtime while our stomachs rumbled, we'd open presents and finally get to eat while the sun was out, but the prize was the big bowl full of candy that Umi would set out for us. Eids last for three days, and Umi would say we could eat all the candy we wanted in that time. But she knew our bodies would reject all that sugar, corn syrup, and starch, and we'd barely make it halfway through the big bowl before jitters, a sugar crash, or a stomach ache made it less appealing. By day two of Eid, we'd be back to our usual snacks like fruit, carrots, celery with peanut butter, boiled eggs, and trail mix.

Umi was playing three-dimensional chess when it came to our health and wellness.

Abu was the community slaughterman and butcher, so when we ate meat, it was often meat that we watched grow up either in the coop in front of or grazing in the fields behind our house. Until one day when we'd come home from school and see it strung up by its feet, headless and skinless. Abu didn't waste anything from the animal; He'd eat livers, gizzards, hearts, brains, tongues, and eyeballs. And the hide might show up again as a Qur'an cover or a Dustacon.

When I started waking up before the rest of the family and knocking on Umi's door to make me breakfast on weekends, she taught me how to make bulgur wheat and malt-o-meal so she could sleep in. Then, when she'd wake up to a filthy kitchen, she taught me how to clean as I cooked. Later in life, I became known for hosting breakfast gatherings. It wasn't because I was trying to be different; it was simply the only kind of food I knew how to cook. I later learned how to use a crock pot and a grill, but I never got around to learning how to make upside down.

Between the organic, farm-to-table, sugar-free, homemade diet Umi had us on and the two to five miles we covered each day going between various clubhouses on our property and friends' houses, we were lean, ripped, and beautiful children. I take no credit when people compliment me on anything physical these days. I got Abu's field negro blood, Umi's cheekbones, and a cheat code childhood, healthwise. But physical health was only one component of the Umi healthcare plan.

Write Now

"Almonds are brain food, you know," Umi said, watching me smash my bag of trail mix.

I was riding shotgun in the Maverick, turning off the unpaved county road 155 onto State Road 554 North toward El Rito. I loved the almond/raisin combination and was hunting them out of my ziplock bag as I tried to chase the banana taste out of my mouth.

"For real?" I asked, intrigued.

"Yes, they're full of vitamin E, which keeps your mind sharp. And raisins are packed with iron, which helps keeps your heart healthy. You have a beautiful mind and a big heart, 2-D. You have to protect them both and use them to do good. You love telling stories, and that's great, but don't tell stories that aren't true when I ask you a question, ok?

I nodded as I chewed on an apricot.

"If you'll lie, you'll steal. If you'll steal, you'll kill."

That got my attention. In my almond-fueled eight-year-old brain, my mother had just drawn a straight line from throwing a banana in the bushes to murder.

She continued, "everyone loves your stories in Ms. Owen's class. If you keep going, you will be a great writer. In your stories, you can be as creative as you want to be."

The saddest part about leaving Abiquiu Elementary was that I had done so well in Ms. Yuvonnia Owen's 3rd Grade class that she invited Umi and me to join her writing club outside school. I was the only kid in the class, but they didn't treat me like one. Once a week, we learned about outlining, dialogue, prose, and story arcs and then read our short stories aloud in front of each other. As a result, one of my stories was adapted into the school play by year's end.

If almonds are brain food and raisins are heart food, reading is writing food. Umi kept us in a library as early as the Fort Worth days. Then, after my near-death experience in the well, she let me go to the library or basketball court connected to the pool while my siblings took swimming lessons. I read for hours, getting lost in other worlds and imagining new ones. The stories, poems, plays, sales copy, and essays that have flowed from my pen since then were all because Umi planted those seeds.

Aftermath

After years of only publishing essays, this book was the ultimate anti-procrastination exercise. Everything was going according to plan until I got stuck when it came time to write about Umi. I knew she would read some of the stories in this book and perceive them as an indictment of the job she did as a mother. But that couldn't be further from the truth.

The central theme of this book is the power of a strong foundation and inspiration. My greatest attributes started as seeds planted by Umi. She imagined who and what I would become long before I could and gave me the tools I would need against all odds. She sacrificed her youth so I could enjoy mine. She instilled principles that enabled me to survive, then thrive in this world. But she still feels bad about some of the events you are about to read about and swears they happened because she divorced Abu.

But I understood all along.

> Umi's entire life was based on serving
> and pleasing other people, despite
> her inquisitive, sensitive nature.

She left Abu because she had to find out who she was beyond taking care of people. So she joined groups like Lifespring and worked in spaces where conscious, free thinkers gathered because that's who she always was. Any version of religion with too much dogma pushed Umi away. Any theology that placed too many barriers between Umi and Allah made her unhealthy. But ultimately, when she came to peace about her place in the world, it still was a place of service. It just had to be on her terms.

Today, she works as a massage therapist for a very niche group. A master of the Dahnhak method after studying in New Jersey and China,

Umi heals her clients by stimulating relaxation points associated with acupressure points, meridians, and body organs. Her work is so thorough that she fills her schedule solely off word of mouth.

She loves watching her lean, ripped, and beautiful grandchildren with her cheekbones, and Abu's Itta Bena blood win State and Regional championships in track. She sends them crocheted afghans and trail mixes in the mail. I wish I could convince her that she did her thing as my mother. She ate all her barakaats and left nothing to clean up behind. She is the Giant in My Midst.

GIANT PRINCIPLE:

You are what you consume. Eat to live, don't live to eat. Instead, feed your mind and body with healthy, clean nourishment. Like sugar becomes fat and fruit becomes energy, thoughts become speech, speech becomes action, actions become habits, and habits become legacy.

Chapter 4:
Zak Abdullah

Made for TV

We didn't watch much TV in New Mexico. Abu being the stickler he was for protecting us from the influence of Shaitaan, meant cable was not an option, and neither was staying inside all day parked in front of a screen.

"Can't even watch a soda commercial without them putting a naked lady in the ice," Abu would tell us. If he remembered anything besides subliminal messaging from his high school advertising class, he kept it to himself.

If my siblings and I were lucky, we'd catch The Fresh Prince on Monday night, The Cosby Show on Thursday night, and cartoons followed by Saved by the Bell on Saturday mornings.

On some Saturdays, I would negotiate with my siblings and parents to fit NBA Inside Stuff into the mix, not wanting to miss an opportunity to watch Ahmad Rashad feature his "main man" of that week. Chances were, I had his main man's basketball card, and it was fascinating to put voices and stories to the names and stats on the cards. Later in the NBA season, NBC would air games on Sunday afternoons, and I became a huge Chicago Bulls fan as they fought to get past the world champion 'Bad Boy' Detroit Pistons. I caught about five Bulls games per year, not including the imaginary ones I played on my dirt court in front of our house.

Umi would blast the theme song to Dallas on Sunday nights as we got into bed, putting a melodic cap on our weekly media intake.

That was TV, though. Films were a different story. A couple of films were considered essential for all Muslim children in the 80s. One was called the Lion of the Desert, and the other was called The Message. Both depicted the life and times of Prophet Muhammad and his companions.

The Ansar

One of the most iconic scenes I have ever seen in a film was from The Message. It showed a part of the Prophet's life that exemplified a verse from the Qur'an that says, "Verily, with hardship comes ease." The Prophet was fleeing persecution from his former tribe along with a group of his followers. Men, women, and children crossed the desert between Mecca and Yathrib on camelback, horseback, and foot. They braved the elements, the emotional shock of separation from their blood and customs, and the threat of ambush from bandits. But their perseverance paid off when they arrived in Yathrib to the rhythmic sound of drums and the singing of a beautiful song called Talaa al Badru Alayna, or The Full Moon Rose Over Us. The Ansars or the Helpers sang the song.

The Ansars were citizens of Yathrib. They were a mix of Christians, Jews, and Muslims who lived harmoniously. They agreed to accept and welcome the Prophet Muhammad because they believed him to fulfill Biblical and Jewish prophecies, which predicted that a Messenger of God would come from the lineage of Abraham's son Ishmael. So not only did they host the Prophet and his people, they welcomed them with open arms and even cleared a path to leadership for Muhammad. The Prophet promptly built a mosque and marketplace and established taxes and laws that were fair and equitable. Muhammad's tenure in Yathrib was so successful that it became known as Madinat Rasul Allah or the City of the Prophet of God. Later the name was shortened to Al Madina or The City.

Yeah, we probably watched The Message 25 times.

The Shed

As I took in the scene under the shed, the bouncing basketballs may as well have been the drums announcing my arrival. The shouts for screens and fouls and kids to get out of the way of the intense full-court game were my welcome song. And though I was that goldfish in a piranha tank, I began to see that I wasn't completely alone. I had some Ansar.

I had never seen anything like the shed before, but it didn't take long for me to figure out its patterns. There were only two goals under the shed, one on the court's north end and another on the south. There were at least 25 grown men and probably 20 kids around my age. Only ten players could play in the game at a time. So the men waiting for their turn on the court would play horseshoes or huddle around someone's truck drinking beers off to the side.

And when the ball traveled to the north side of the court, the ten kids on the south side rushed onto the court to get shots up before the game came back down. When the game went to the south side, the south side shooters scattered to the sidelines while the north side shooters flooded their side of the court. The name of the game for the kids was to take makable shots, so you never got caught chasing down a long rebound when the actual game was coming back down to your side. Disrupting the real game could result in getting run over, cussed out, or getting your ball kicked into the adjacent baseball field. If the wrong player ran into you, you could get all three.

After peeping the rules and feeling comfortable with my ability to follow suit, I decided to join the south siders for a shift. I grabbed a rebound, sprinted to the top of the key, and splashed a jumper. Then, feeling good about the first impression I must have made with onlookers, I looked behind me and saw the game coming back down to the south side of the court. So I turned and sprinted to the sideline. Just as I did, I felt something whiz past my head and heard, "Ball ball ball ball!!!"

The game had come to a halt because the ball I'd shot had hit the point guard, and he was livid.

"Which one of yall little niggas hit me with this?" The man demanded, with the game ball held to his left hip by his forearm and the loose ball on his right palm. It was my first time hearing the word nigga in real life.

The team captain who had next pointed at a kid standing on the baseline. It was the same kid whose rebound I had grabbed before I took my shot. His name was Perry. The point guard walked to within 10 feet of Perry, screaming, "If yo ass is too stupid to hold the ball when we coming down, stay off the GODDAMN COURT!!"

The man fired the wayward ball at Perry's legs. The ball skipped past Perry, and he ran to retrieve the ball and escape the embarrassment of having dozens of eyeballs cast shame upon him for breaking the golden rule.

The game continued, and Perry returned to the sideline, fighting tears and staring at me with a scowl. I thought he was jealous because I made my shot, and he missed his. These piranhas were strange.

When the game ended, we kids took over both sides of the court while the next team figured out the plan for their upcoming match against the winners. Most of the crowd centered around one kid who had just finished playing on the losing team. No wonder he was the center of attention; he was an 11-year-old kid who had just held his own in a hyper-competitive game with skilled adults. And now his friends were showing him love for holding it down on all of our behalves.

His name was Zakariyyah Abdullah, but everyone called him Zak.

He was tall with curly brown hair, huge brown eyes, and a mouth full of big straight teeth that never stopped running. All of his facial features were perfectly symmetrical. He seemed to always be smiling, talking, or both while cracking jokes. His confidence in the game carried right over into how he handled himself off the court. He reminded me of a mashup between Zack Morris from Saved by the Bell and Will Smith from The Fresh Prince.

I made it a point to guard Zak as we shot around and blocked the first shot he attempted against me, a baseline jumper. His face lit up after that, and the trash talk commenced.

"Where the hell did this guy come from?" Zak said, laughing.

As he said it, he caught his rebound, stepped back, and splashed an even deeper shot with my hand in his face.

"Gimme my change!" he yelled, walking to the top of the key with me shadowing him. The ball zipped back into his hands.

"Oh, you get the ball back if you make your shot?" I asked.

"Yeah, you get your change. But not on layups."

I glanced at Perry standing under the basket, waiting for a rebound, and felt a little guilty. I now understood why he was mad; he was trying to give me my change, and I didn't catch his return pass after making the jumper.

We went back and forth for a few shots, with Zak ramping up his intensity as I began to show I could play a little.

"Nah, but for real, where you from?" He eventually asked.

"New Mexico," I replied in a low tone.

Zak burst out laughing. "Mexico?? You don't look Mexican…You for real?"

I corrected him, "no, NEW Mexico. The state."

It didn't matter. All the other kids had laughed with Zak, and none of them caught my correction.

"Lil Mexico think he can hoop. Y'all had basketball out there?"

It was Perry. He was crowding me, his chin almost touching my collarbone and speaking through the same scowl he'd flashed in my direction earlier. I had sensed good-natured teasing in my interaction with Zak, but this felt different.

Just then, the winning team returned to the court, signaling the beginning of a new game, and the adhan began to call from the masjid up the hill. I'd heard the adhan countless times growing up Muslim, but this was the first time I experienced its intended effect. Around seven men and nearly all of the boys dropped everything and began making their way up the hill to the masjid to make Asr, the late afternoon prayer the third of five Muslims make daily.

I lagged, wanting to keep Perry in my sight.

Zak stayed with me and put his arm around my shoulder, saying, "Some of these dudes are gonna try you, but as soon as you show them you're not scared, they'll leave you alone."

I nodded, heart pounding.

We prayed, and when we returned to the court, the full court five on fives had stopped. The Muslim exodus must have taken the wind out of the court's sails. So we started a game of 21, which I also had never played.

21 is a game that pits every player against the field. A player has to get the ball by rebounding a missed shot or stealing the ball from another player. If you score, you get two points, then you go to the "free throw" line, which was the top of the key - far enough away to be a high school three-pointer. If you make the first free throw, you get a second. If you make the second, you get a third. If you make the third free throw, you get the ball back, but now you have to try to score another two-pointer against the field.

Usually, at the beginning of 21, only one defender goes out to guard the player with the ball. There are two reasons for this. First, most people are more focused on rebounding a missed shot so they can get their turn to score. So they prefer to jockey for rebounding position under the basket instead of wasting energy chasing a player on defense. And second, if you play too aggressively on defense, it almost guarantees you'll have a motivated defender whenever you get a chance to score. If you play tough defense on five different players, those same five can swarm you when it's your turn with the ball. Unlike team basketball, there is no one to pass the ball to in 21. So once a player reaches 15 points, he'll likely be swarmed by multiple players because they'll be motivated to stop him from getting to 21 points and winning the game.

Zak started the game by making a long jumper and three free throws. He got the ball back, laughed at the two defenders who sprinted out to guard him, pump-faked, blew past them both, and pulled up to sink a mid-range jumper just before reaching the crowd under the basket. He made his first two free throws and finally missed the last one.

Zak was already up 9-0 on everyone, so I went hard for the rebound, showing off my daily hike hops. But as soon as I touched the ball at my apex, I felt my legs taken from under me. I came off balance and had to stick my right hand down to brace for contact with the concrete, sacrificing my hand, forearm, and shoulder to protect my head.

I lay there for a second to see if I was seriously hurt, but everything felt ok. Then, I looked up and saw Perry standing over me, laughing.

"Yeah nigga" he said simply.

This was the ghetto stuff I was afraid of.

I stood up, dusted myself off, and Perry got into a fighting stance. A circle formed around us. I looked at Zak as if to say, "aren't you going to do something to stop this?" His return glare said, "remember what I told you. You have to fight your own battles."

So I began to size Perry up. He was my height but considerably skinnier than I was. He didn't seem to have much support for his actions; these kids just wanted a show.

I learned how to fight by having a hyper-aggressive brother 11 months older than me. I idolized Mike Tyson growing up, and because of Abu's no-hitting in-the-face rule, I perfected his low hook to the rib cage when Yaseen, who preferred to wrestle, would charge me. But Yaseen was bigger and stronger and would inevitably get me to the ground, where I also had to learn how to be effective.

This kid Perry didn't stand a chance against me, I thought.

"I don't want to fight you," I said, studying his unbalanced stance. "Sorry I didn't catch the ball!"

"Mexico scaaared!" Perry said, laughing. "Nah nigga, you bout to get yo ass whooped." He walked off the court into the grass and put his fists up.

"If you step in the grass, I'm going in your grill!"

At this point, I wanted it to be over, so I went to the grass. Perry swung and missed my head with a wild haymaker. I caught him by his waist and slung him to the ground. Everybody went crazy.

"Oh snap! Ok, Mexico!!"

Perry was livid, but everyone fell silent when the tall man from the top of the hill walked up on the fray. He looked at Zak. "Who started it, man?" Zak gestured toward Perry. The man looked at me. "You ok?" I nodded. "This game is over. Perry, meet me at the bench."

On the walk back to the Cherokee, I learned that the man was Imam Jamil Al-Amin, formerly known as H. Rap Brown. I also learned that I had made some friends by standing up to Perry because most of the crowd was walking with me, giddily recapping what had just happened.

When we reached the car, Abu and Umi talked to a man named Brother Hasan Abdullah and a woman named Sister Fatima Abdullah. I couldn't help but look at Sister Fatima and think she would fit better in Abiquiu. She was a white lady with a khimar and loose-fitting clothes, and she was clearly in her element among all these people who looked nothing like her. Zak walked up to her and kissed her on the cheek as we piled into the Cherokee.

"I see you met Zakariyyah. I knew you would get along with him." Umi said.

"How do you know Zak?" I asked.

"We'll live with them for a little while until we find a house." She replied.

A smile crept up my face.

Shadow

Over the next few weeks, I was Zak's shadow, studying everything from how he spoke with his half Philly, part Pittsburg, part Atlanta accent to how he dressed and acted. Zak was the consummate charmer and could get his way because he was genuine, persistent, and funny. Even when he wasn't amusing, Zak would laugh and laugh until the laugh became what was funny. We would walk from their house on our dead-end block around the West End, and Zak would show me how to move around the drug dealers, the killers, and the girls. He was the perfect ambassador to the ghetto. And I soaked it all up.

When my father found a house two weeks later, it was directly across the street from Zak and the Abdullah clan of nine. The Abdullahs were the perfect Ansars to us, and our families became inseparable. When Sister Fatima had more children, they saw our house as a quieter alternative that they could escape to for naps. When we were out of food stamps, we borrowed theirs and vice versa. When Zak needed another man for a late-night game of three-on-three behind our neighbor's house, he knew he could tap on my window, and I would sneak out of it to join them.

When Zak's AAU team, the Atlanta Celtics, needed a scorekeeper, I was the perfect choice because I was at all the games and a basketball stat junkie anyway. The Celtics would later become famous when Zak's coach Prather landed Dwight Howard and Josh Smith, but Zak was a phenomenal athlete in his own right. Even in a starting lineup that included future NBA player Jamison Brewer, Zak's athleticism and shooting ability made him the crowd favorite, and the sky seemed to be his limit.

A Foot in the Street

Zak's brothers' and friends' influence grew stronger on Zak as we got older. One day while hanging out near some known dope houses, a car pulled up on Zak, and the passenger fired on him, hitting him multiple times in the legs. Not long after healing from the shooting, Zak found himself a passenger in a car driven by a couple of known gangsters. They pulled up to Zak's house to drop him off when they got a call that made them hastily pull off. But not before Zak had cleared the car. He still had one foot on the sidewalk and another in the street. The driver ran over Zak's leg twice, breaking it in several places.

Zak's athleticism never returned, and any hoops dreams that the hood had for him died while he was recovering with his leg elevated on Sister Fatima's couch.

Zak's adult life took some twists and turns — you could say he kept one foot on the sidewalk and another in the street long after his leg healed up. As a result, he had some brushes with the law and some very tough brushes with death. But they didn't break him.

Aftermath

Zak is more stoic and measured these days, but he still has charm and good looks and has built himself into a master salesman. Today, he lives in Seattle and could probably sell fish to the anglers there.

I'm forever grateful for **Zakariyyah Abdullah.**
He taught me hospitality.
He taught me finesse.
He taught me how to survive.
He was a true Ansar and a Giant in My Midst.

GIANT PRINCIPLE:

Welcome new people as Zak welcomed me to the Shed. A true star is confident nothing can dim its light. There is room for everyone to shine.

Chapter 5:
Khalfani Adair

Bidah School

I could not tell the story of my evolution from goldfish to piranha without Khalfani Adair.

The first day Yaseen and I walked into At-Taqwa Academy on Delowe Drive, we scanned the room and saw one student out of 20 who looked like he might be old enough and cool enough to kick it with. He was a tall, dark, slim kid with waves and a quick, broad smile. But he had a mysteriousness to him. We had been in Atlanta for three years, and he seemed like he would fit in with our other friends from the West End, but we had never seen him. Nonetheless, we bonded quickly.

Mainly via mutual rebellion.

As our teacher, Brother Muhammad, went over the rules and expectations for the startup school, Yaseen, Khalfani, and I made incredulous faces at each other the entire time. On Brother Muhammad's list of forbidden things were fades and parts in our hair, pants that hung below the waist or ankle, and shorts, amongst many other seemingly innocent things.

You see, Brother Muhammad was a "Salafi." The term comes from the salaf al-Salih, the first three generations of Muslims. Brother Muhammad and the Salafis believed those first three generations represented the purest form of Islam and should be emulated by all Muslims, regardless of time or context. Not only in their beliefs but also in their practices and dress. To them, the ways to fight against unbelief and idol worship (shirk) were by encouraging and teaching Muslims to remove innovative beliefs and practices (bid'ah).

I don't think Abu knew it when he enrolled us. Still, At-Taqwa Academy was Brother Muhammad's way of teaching the youth the methods of the Salafi and saving us from the evil influences of America.

We didn't know about Salafism then because it was just starting to spread along the East coast. But we quickly learned what bid'ah was, according to Brother Muhammad. To us, it seemed like everything we liked was either haram (forbidden) or bid'ah to Brother Muhammad. So privately, we began calling him Bidah Man and At-Taqwa Academy Bidah School. To us, Bidah Man was a villain who needed to under-stand life was not lived on paper. Especially not documents written in Saudi Arabia centuries ago.

Jumping Fresh

It was 1994. I was 12, Yaseen was 13, and Khalfani was 14 or 15. His age was always a bit of a mystery. Either way, we were in the throes of early adolescence in Atlanta, Georgia, during the dawn of a hip-hop explosion in the city. At-Taqwa Academy was only one mile from the intersection of Headland and Delowe, which was made famous a couple of years later by a line in an Outkast song.

It was terrible enough that our parents sent us to this small school in a house with a bunch of little boys. But there was no way Brother Muhammad expected us to ride the 83 Campbellton Road from Oak-land City station to Campbellton and Delowe with lame hair and high-water pants. If we did, we would get roasted mercilessly by the Therrell High school kids on the 83.

I had learned the power of attraction from Zak. I saw firsthand how much more he got out of life because of how handsome he was and how he leveraged it. I was starting to come into my looks a little, even developing a little peach fuzz. So Umi's crocheted and kente cloth kufis were beginning to be left at home more and more. And Abu's one style in his barber repertoire — the baldy with patches — was no longer an option.

For kids my age in early 90s Atlanta, being well groomed and well dressed was not mere vanity. Instead, it was a defense mechanism against bullying. The less a kid had "wrong" with his haircut, clothes, or shoes, the less negative attention he brought upon himself. In the home of "jonin," just for kicks, getting fresh was another survival tactic.

And I was collecting those.

So the first time I made a little money working for Abu, shortly after starting Bidah School, I bought a black Bulls Starter jacket with corduroy sleeves and got my first professional haircut.

My first barber was a man named Bill from Detroit. He was the second chair at Melvin's barbershop, two blocks from the West End Mosque on Ralph David Abernathy Boulevard. Bill seemed to relish the opportunity to help me figure out my swag. He peeped my Bulls jacket when I hung it up and promptly booed.

"We got a Bulls fan! Let me guess; you want the shiny bald look?"

He reached for his straight razor. I laughed and thought about all the haircuts I admired through the years, from Will Smith and his cousin Carlton to Kid from Kid N' Play. But what popped out of my mouth was, "Gimme the Scottie Pippen."

Scottie was best known as the long-armed, deep-voiced, and long-nosed sidekick to Michael Jordan, so it fit with the Bulls reference.

Bill nodded and said, "Ok, I can see that. Scottie is a dog." Then he got to work.

I walked out of Melvin's, feeling like a new man. When Bill showed me my first cut in his handheld mirror, I barely recognized the face looking back at me. Somehow, it made me look older, more handsome, and cleaner. Haircuts were sorcery, and I have sworn by them since.

When I got home, I noticed Bill had nicked my right eyebrow while shaping up my hairline. Back then, my line was abnormally close to my eyebrows. Not wanting it to look like a mistake, I found Abu's clipper set, pulled out the ones that looked like Bill's shape-up clippers, and decided to finish the job.

Wildin Out

I walked into Bidah School the next day, looking like Big Daddy Kane with three cuts in my right eyebrow to match my perfect high-top fade. All the boys gasped and started laughing and pointing while distributing their collective gaze between Brother Muhammad and me. He was in the middle of his morning routine, which included a speech that Prophet Muhammad would recite before his sermons.

When done, Brother Muhammad looked at me and said, "Masood, stand up."

My giddy little classmates said, "oooooh!"

I stood up, looking at Brother Muhammad with a straight face.

"Look at him." Brother Muhammad said to the younger students. "This is how silly you look when you imitate the kuffar!"

I shifted but kept a straight face, staring at brother Muhammad with my jaw clenched while he addressed my peers.

"Masood is as smart as, if not smarter than, anyone here. But he decided to look like people who will be fuel for the Hellfire. How smart is that?"

At that moment, I decided to defy Brother Muhammad at every turn. If I was the example of a bad kid, I would be the best example, dammit.

The next day, I walked into the morning session and noticed something different about Khalfani. He had gotten a haircut but was covering it poorly with one of those flimsy white kufis that still have the fold marks. It was the first time I'd seen him in a kufi. I sat down next to him and put my face two inches from the back of his head while he tried to ignore me. He had gotten a fade! I pulled my face around so he could see my eyeballs, which were as wide as I could get them to stretch. Finally, he grinned and turned his face toward me with a look that told me to chill out. But when he did, I saw three cuts in his eyebrow. Khalfani is wildin out with me, I thought. This guy gets it!

Khalfani refused to take his kufi off when Brother Muhammad asked him to, saying he tried to cut his own hair but messed it up and was too embarrassed. So Khalfani had just made himself public enemy number two to my public enemy number one.

Over the next few months at Bidah School, Khalfani, Yaseen, and I continued to push the limits of rebellion. Technically, we weren't even that bad at school. We just kept getting our hair faded, cutting our eyebrows, and rapping at lunchtime.

Rap music was strictly haram in Brother Muhammad's book, but we didn't care. Khalfani and I would write verses inspired by Tupac or Bone Thugs N Harmony, while Yaseen provided the beatboxing and an occasional verse inspired by the Wu-Tang Clan. There was something about hip-hop that felt like therapy for the things we were experiencing growing up in the hood.

We also started pushing back on some of Brother Muhammad's Salafi ideologies. A typical exchange would be:

Brother Muhammad: ...and that's how germs spread viruses. Does anyone have any questions?

Me: *Raises hand*

BM: Yes, Masood.

Me: If everything related to Islam that the Prophet didn't do is bid'ah, isn't it bid'ah to drive to the Masjid to make salat under the electric lights?

BM: Does anyone have any questions related to the topic of germs?

Khalfani: *Raises hand*

BM: Yes, Khalfani?

Khalfani: The Prophet didn't have soap, so isn't it bid'ah for you to use soap when you take a ghusl or make wudhu? I saw some soap in your bathroom, so...

Yaseen: Yeah, isn't it bid'ah to use toilet paper to wipe your butt when you make istinjah? Because the Prophet didn't have toilet paper...

Eventually, Brother Muhammad ran out of patience, lecture material, or both, and Khalfani and I kept turning in A+ work, so we silently but mutually agreed to back off each other. Eventually, Bidah School wasn't so bad.

But on MARTA to and from school and the weekends, it was a different and more dangerous story.

F What's Right

Khalfani was born Marquis Cortez Adair in Compton, California. He grew up in a neighborhood where he earned the nickname KC Locc. His preferred style of dress was khaki, black, or navy blue Dickies with a white, blue, or black t-shirt and a pair of Chuck Taylors. Think of a cooler, smarter Smokey from the movie Friday. He sometimes wore baggy blue jeans, and in the winter, he had a royal blue, black and white Toronto Maple Leafs Starter coat that I loved and always tried to borrow to no avail. For one, he couldn't fit my Bulls jacket, and for two, he never, under any circumstances, wore red.

When Khalfani told stories outside of school, I got the sense that he had seen levels of violence that I'd only read about or seen in movies. When he told them, his eyes made you wonder if he was just a witness for them all.

After school and on weekends, the MARTA cards that our parents bought us still worked. That meant we could go for free anywhere in the city we pleased. It also meant spending a lot of time on trains and buses.

One day on a northbound train from West End station, Khalfani pulled out a large Sharpie and began to draw STK in graffiti-style letters on a posted ad. Beneath that, he wrote FWR. Stunned and impressed by Khalfani's boldness, Yaseen and I looked at each other, and finally, Yaseen asked what it stood for.

Khalfani said, "Shoot to Kill."

"And what's FWR?" I asked.

"F What's Right," Khalfani replied, matter of factly.

I took the marker and wrote "WEA" in an exaggerated, angular font on the top left corner. Each letter encroached upon the space of the others.

"Ok!" Khalfani said, grinning. "What's that stand for?"

"West End Assassins," I replied, remembering what some of the gangster Muslim boys in the West End had recently begun calling themselves.

I was no assassin, but I was cool with them, so I felt like an honorary member of sorts. The vandalism gave me a rush of adrenaline.

Over the next two years, our petty little acts of rebellion mounted, but two incidents eradicated whatever goldfish I still had in me. Both times, Khalfani was involved.

Straight Hustled

One summer payday, I decided to go on a solo mission to Lenox Mall to buy some shoes and clothes. I did my shopping, hopped on the Southbound train, and put my best mean mug on in case anyone saw the bags and wanted to try something. I was in luck; the car I was in was thug free.

I got off at West End station and sat on one of the granite benches between where the 67 Westview and 71 Cascade parked. Either bus would get me home, but neither was there. As I waited, a smiling man wearing clothes similar to those I had just bought approached me and said, "Ok, I see you out here getting fresh, young nigga!"

I looked around and then back at him from toe to head twice, stoned-faced. Finally, his smile widened, seemingly appreciating that I was also a serious individual that you didn't want to just run up on.

"I don't mean no harm, bruh!" He said, grinning with his hands in the air, the universal sign for don't shoot me. "You just remind me of myself when I was your age. What are you, 16, 17?"

"13," I replied. But looking older was one of the best compliments anyone could pay me at the time, so it made me relax a little with the man, who appeared to be around 25.

Motioning toward my bags, he said, "Damn… you 13 getting it in like this? You a straight hustler!" He reached his hand out for some dap. I compromised with an extended fist, and he settled for the bump.

"You pay full price for all this?" He asked, sitting on the arm of the bench.

I scooted away and looked at him.

"What's up, man? I don't know you."

He nodded, looked around, and said in a lower voice, "I feel that. But nah, it's just… I got a connect on the clothes. If you didn't spend all your money, I could probably get you twice what you have now for half the price. My man be having Jays, Timbs, Polo, Tommy, Cybertek, whatever. You like Jordans?"

"Who don't like Jays?" I replied.

"That's what I'm saying!" He said, laughing. "You trying to get all the way fresh for school?"

"Hell yeah," I said.

"What time you gotta be back home?" He asked. "We'd have to go up by North Avenue."

"I'm straight. I ain't worried about that." I said, trying to maintain my 16 or 17 vibe.

"Alright bet, let's go."

I followed the man up the stairs, and we got on a Northbound train. He told me the clothes plug was a booster who was so good at it that he paid for two condos in the same building. He lived in one, but the other one was for merchandise. So when we got to North Avenue station, he called the booster from a pay phone.

When the man returned, he said, "We gotta go to the condo he lives in because he has some people shopping right now and doesn't let clients meet each other. Shouldn't take long."

It sounded like reasonable criminal activity to me, so we walked from North Avenue to a condo not far from the station and waited.

The man turned on ESPN and asked if I wanted something to drink.

"Nah, I'm straight," I replied. "How long you think it's gonna be?"

"I know, right? I thought he would've been called by now. Let me run over there real quick and see what's up," he said and walked out the front door.

It was only then that my mind started appraising how vulnerable I was at the moment.

What if this is a robbery? I thought.

I don't know this dude's name, no one knows where I am, and I have all these brand-new clothes on me. I started to walk around the condo, looking for potential weapons and escapes. After a few minutes, my nerves were so bad that I grabbed my bags and walked to the front door just as the man walked back in, smiling. "My bad, bruh, it's just gonna be a few more minutes."

"I'm just gonna head out, man," I said.

"Oh nah, don't do that. What happened that quick?" He asked, moving toward me.

I told the truth. "I don't know you, and it seems like you're playing games."

"Psssh! What? Play games? Maaan, we *do* this!" The man pulled out a wad of cash. "Chill out. You won't regret it!"

Ruling out robbery thanks to the cash, I exhaled and said, "I have five more minutes, then I have to go home."

"Oh, your mama got you on a curfew?" The man was positioned between me and the door and stepped closer still, around a glass coffee table.

"Pssh… nah. I'm just not feeling this."

I was lying about the curfew. I was supposed to be home by Maghrib. But I was telling the truth about not feeling the situation.

The man's energy shifted from cool to desperate.

"Just wait a few minutes… here, you can hold this if it makes you feel better." He peeled off three $100 bills and walked up to hand them to me.

Then a demonic look arrived in his eyes, and he said, almost pleading, "I'll give you the whole stack if you let me go down on you while we wait."

He said it with a serpent's hiss and in more vulgar terms.

Confused and embarrassed, I shoved him into the coffee table, sending him tumbling backward and through the glass. I grabbed my bags, ran as fast as possible out of the condo, and didn't stop until I reached North Avenue station.

I was out of breath, shocked, and felt so naive. My mind was racing.

Do I look gay?

What am I putting out there that made him think I would do that?

Am I that gullible?

How many young dudes take the money?

I could have died.

I could have killed him.

I *should* have killed him…

I never told anyone about that incident. Instead, I vented to Khalfani the next day about how many gay dudes were starting to turn up in the city. I made up a story about a bunch of them harassing me that didn't make me sound like a total goldfish. He was down to start checking them with me. If STK/FWR was a gang, homosexuals had just become our opps.

For the rest of the summer, if we encountered a gay-looking man who glanced in our direction, I would lash out and embarrass him. One man lived at the end of our block across from Zak's house and wore long wigs and women's clothes. He never said anything to us or bothered anyone, but I started throwing rocks in his direction when I saw him coming home from work.

Steady Mobbing

Adrenaline is a drug. And like any drug, eventually intimidating and embarrassing didn't satisfy my craving for adrenaline or repudiation. I needed bigger fixes. So we would mob up to Piedmont Park, where many gay men were starting to frequent. We would walk three across and block their paths on the sidewalks, looking for a fight. If one of them bumped into one of us, looked too long, or said the wrong thing, it got ugly quickly.

In my traumatized adolescent mind, these guys didn't dare to push their predators through the coffee table as I did, so they took the money and what came with it and got possessed by the gay demon. I was a crusader sent to beat that demon out of them.

I justified my actions as many religious people do with the story of Lot in the Bible and Qur'an. I wasn't throwing rocks at my neighbor; I was *stoning* him. Khalfani didn't seem to need any justification. He was going to ride for his friend, regardless.

Jihadul Grady

My time to repay Khalfani for his loyalty came that winter. Khalfani had gotten a job at Kroger that summer and had fallen for one of his fellow cashiers, a girl named Tasha.

Dating in the traditional American sense is strictly prohibited in Islam, so when things got serious between them, Khalfani and Tasha had to immediately consider marriage for it to be a lawful courtship in Khalfani's mother's eyes. Tasha even became Muslim and chose to begin covering her hair.

Some boys who'd known Tasha since elementary school did not take her conversion to Islam seriously. On Valentine's Day of 10th grade, they cornered her at her locker and pulled off her khimar, prompting a hysterical phone call to her "intendant" Khalfani on her lunch break. So Khalfani met Tasha at North Avenue station with flowers and asked her to point out the bullies. He then walked calmly up to them in front of nearly every train-riding Grady student in the station and told them that if they touched Tasha again, it would not end well for them.

These boys were from Techwood Homes and Bedford Pines in the 4th Ward, parts of town equally as tough as the West End.

The following day the bullies cornered Tasha and snatched off her khimar again. While throwing it to the ground, one of the boys said, "tell your little Muzzlim boyfriend!"

So she did.

And he told Yaseen and me, and I told Zak and some of my West End Assassin homies. So we mobbed nine deep up to Grady High School for what, to us, was jihad. Regardless of where we came from — Compton, Alabama, New Mexico, Ohio, Philadelphia, or Atlanta — the concept of protecting our Muslim Sisters was instilled in us very young. And pulling off a khimar — any khimar — was a declaration of war.

We gathered across the street from Grady's football Stadium at a shopping plaza and got word to some people we knew at Grady that Khalfani and Yaseen were back to fight Tasha's bullies in the parking lot after school. Those two were to stand in plain view while the rest of us hid strategically behind cars and pillars around the plaza and parking lot.

The plan worked.

The main bully, a kid ironically named Cortez, wielding an umbrella as a weapon, had gathered four of his friends to jump Khalfani and Yaseen. Khalfani played his role to the fullest, raising both hands to the sky in the universal "What's Good?" stance when he saw Cortez and crew cross the street.

A small crowd was following the boys from Grady, anxious to see them beat down the two bold Muslim boys. But as they neared the unfazed Khalfani and Yaseen, we began to emerge from our posts, surrounding the group and moving in with speed. Then, recognizing they were outnumbered, three boys ran for it, barreling through the wall we'd built, Red Rover style.

Cortez did the same after seeing his backup run, splitting from his friend. "Don't let these two get away!" Khalfani yelled, pointing at Cortez and his co-bully. He made it across the street before getting hunted down and punished by Khalfani and Yaseen on the corner of 10th and Monroe.

I pursued the other guy with one of the Assassins, catching him on the corner of 8th and Monroe and delivering countless Tyson-inspired blows to his body, followed by ill-intended uppercuts while he wrestled with the Assassin. I stopped when he crumbled to the sidewalk, but my cohort kept stomping him, led by a rage far more significant than my own, until I hugged him and told him it was enough.

I looked around to assess the scene and saw that a couple of Assassins had caught one of the first three to flee and were delivering a similar punishment to him.

Girls were screaming.

Cars were stopping and honking on Monroe Drive.

People asked if the three victims were alive or dead as they writhed in pain on the cold concrete.

Rain began to fall.

A Grady student brought Cortez one of his shoes, which somehow had landed over the fence which separated Monroe Drive from the football field.

All nine of us boarded the 27 Monroe and watched the scene get smaller as the bus pulled away. Cortez's girlfriend was on the bus, crying and shaking in fear. We comforted her and assured her he would be ok.

Zak got her number.

Infamy

That night, all my friends who went to Grady or the affiliated Sutton Middle School up the street called me with a version of what happened after school, each more exaggerated than the next.

Whether it was "I heard y'all were 50 deep" or "I heard you knocked out three 11th graders by yourself," it fed my ego.

Beating up effeminate men and their boyfriends had started to feel like bullying and, thus, unsatisfying. But this was different. I felt infamous, like an antihero.

Riding this high, Yaseen, Khalfani, and I decided to meet Tasha and her friend Joan, who was also considering becoming Muslim, at Grady the next day. Of course, we did so under the guise of protecting them from any blowback from the melee the day before, but it was a victory lap. For me, at least.

We walked through the after-school crowds for the second day in a row, but this time we were celebrities. Boys cleared the way, nodded, and girls stood in the way, showed off their dimples, and batted their eyelashes. We left the campus from the same direction Cortez and company had approached us the previous day, crossing Monroe into the plaza parking lot.

"Oh no." Tasha and Joan said in unison while pausing in their tracks no sooner than I got two feet into the parking lot.

"What?" Khalfani asked, on alert.

"That's Cortez's big brother," Joan said worriedly. "He graduated last year."

Across the parking lot on the Mellow Mushroom Pizza's patio, a tall young man was rising from his chair and squinting in our direction as four other guys, three of whom I recognized as the Red Rover escapees, stood up behind him and pointed in our direction.

"Man, let's dip," Yaseen said.

Khalfani straightened his back to flex his entire 6'3" frame, placed his heels within three inches of each other, with his toes pointing in opposite directions, and raised both hands high above his head, again striking the "What's Good?" stance. This time, he had no umbrella, strategy, or secret Assassins. It didn't matter; we were walking full speed toward a much more difficult fight with much less help.

We spent much time at Khalfani's house playing Street Fighter II when we weren't kicking up dust. As we approached the hostile group, I heard the announcer's voice in my head: "Round. Two. FIGHT!!

Yaseen heard something else in his. Maybe some smooth jazz or a Martin Luther King speech about nonviolence.

Because by the time we approached the quintet of Cortez's pissed-off friends and family, Yaseen had decided to use reason and debate, attempting to convince the group that we could settle our differences amicably.

Walking up to one of the guys with his palms turned up and saying something about squashing it, Yaseen caught a vicious blow to the jaw from another guy positioned behind him and crumbled to the ground. Like that, we were down our best fighter, outnumbered 5-2.

Khalfani swung on Cortez's brother, connecting with two blows before getting wrapped up by the one who'd hit Yaseen and moved into the parking lot.

Stunned by Yaseen's lifeless-looking body bleeding on the sidewalk and outnumbered three to one, I sensed that I might die if I did not make the right moves over the next minute or so.

I was easily the youngest and smallest person in the fight, and they weren't attacking me with the same urgent force that they had, Yaseen or Khalfani, so I backed off the sidewalk into the more spacious parking lot. Then I got on my toes as they attacked.

I can't pretend to remember how I survived that—Probably Umi's prayers.

I knew I took some blows, gave some back, and didn't fall. But, more than anything, I outlasted them. Perhaps it was those daily five-mile hikes in Abiquiu kicking in.

Somehow, out of the corner of my eye, I saw that Khalfani was much more vulnerable than I was.

One of the two young men he was fighting had him pinned down by his arms against the open bed of a pickup truck while the other was fitting something shiny between his knuckles, apparently to shank Khalfani in the abdomen.

Escaping from my three tired opponents without much resistance, I made my way toward Khalfani. En route, I saw another pickup truck with two-by-four wooden planks in the back. I grabbed one about three or four feet long, and just as the guy with the shank cocked his fist back to shove the shiny object into Khalfani's gut, I swung the two-by-four as hard as I could, hitting him in the back of his head.

The sound of pine against skull was deafening. The commotion of the second brawl in as many days in that parking lot halted, the sound of the shank hitting the ground signaling its end.

The carpenter whose two-by-four I had taken angrily gathered his piece of wood off the ground and let us know that he'd called the police, thereby ending the fight.

Khalfani and I rushed to Yaseen, who was regaining consciousness. But he was bleeding from a nasty scrape on his face, sustained when he hit the cement. The other group rallied around the guy I'd dropped with the two-by-four. I never looked back to see how he was.

Aftermath

Khalfani and I both mellowed as we got older and remained friends well into adulthood. We competed for the unofficial title of "Best Rapper out of the West End" in our late teens and early twenties with various projects that he and I would release and perform for our circles of friends. However, I think Lil Baby may have surpassed us now.

Khalfani later began to host an event called the Poetry Forum near the Atlanta University Center that would help introduce me to my wife.

When one of our mutual dream girls from those early days hinted that she wanted something like what my wife and I had, I helped steer her in Khalfani's direction, then helped him say the right things to seal the deal. My rationale? He was the most similar person I had ever known, except maybe smarter.

The times Khalfani and I had in 1994, and 1995 showed me a side of me that I needed to know existed. I always thought I was 90% Umi and 10% Abu, but those FWR/STK days showed I had quite a bit of Lil Mo' in me. Temper was a beast that I would need to tame, and my lack of empathy was something to watch. But more importantly, I moved through the world with much more confidence and swag, knowing I could always protect myself. I just needed to make sure I was using my powers for good.

Khalfani Adair is a Certified Forensic Interrogator in the financial crime sector and a freelance photographer these days.

Like Zak, he has settled in the northwest and leads a life opposite the one we had to survive.

He taught me to be brave.
He taught me I could challenge authority.
He taught me to stand up for those I love at all costs.
He taught me how to hunt piranhas.
He was a Giant in My Midst.

GIANT PRINCIPLE:

Confront life before life confronts you.

Chapter 6:
Abdullah Rabbani

Broken Halos

Growing up in the West End in the 1990s, we Muslim kids had a halo. Thanks to the efforts of Imam Jamil Al-Amin and his Sutra, or community security team, that halo got us a free pass on the usual peer pressure that came with growing up in a drug-infested neighborhood.

We could walk past the dope boys without being recruited and past the hookers without being solicited. The dice game might pause for a hot second if they sensed us getting too curious. But that was about it.

The halo didn't work regarding what we saw or how we processed it.

If anything, its glow gave our nafs (worldly desires) a built-in spotlight. Some older boys traded their halos for street fame after getting a little freedom. There was an extra edge on the name in the street when it was Rakim or Ali. The Ricos and Jasons of the world were lost causes, but Rakim and Ali were supposed to be better. So their 'bad' was *really* bad because they had to fight so many built-in layers of protection to arrive at those poor choices.

A group of these types formed and began to exercise a brand of vigilante justice on the dope boys in our community. They were the aforementioned West End Assassins. My proximity to the Assassins and cues from certain hip-hop artists made the idea of the thug life appealing. In addition, my exploits with Khalfani gave me a taste of the adrenaline rushes and infamy that came with violence and rebellion. What unsupervised angry teen doesn't like adrenaline rushes or popularity?

When Assassins came down to our dead-end part of the street at night, I would sneak out and hang around to listen to stories about their exploits.

Most of them were a lot like me, the embodiment of anti-establishment.

Rebellion was in our blood, and our fathers ensured we knew what we were against. We weren't exactly sure what we were *for*, though.

Many of the baby boomer Black American Muslim men who raised us were anti-secular schools, anti-law enforcement, anti-banks, anti-legal marriage, anti-corporate America, and anti-worshippers of white Jesus.

They were pro "doing for self," which, for many in the early nineties, had become a catch-all for being a slightly off-grid solopreneur, no matter what your expertise may have been. That often meant no health, dental, or life insurance. No savings, no 401k. Just Allah and his Rasul. That's all you need.

The collective trauma and baggage incurred by the Black American community via the Vietnam war and the Civil Rights movement were extensive. So it wasn't hard to understand why they would want us to distrust the government. However, because positivity motivates me more than negativity, building an identity off of what I was against was a chore.

My general disposition was, "Yes, that happened. Now what?"

Don't like secular schools? Understandable. But replace it with a comprehensive school that teaches me a bankable skill.

Don't want us to cooperate or trust law enforcement? I understood that too. Teach us to secure our community and avoid trouble with the law.

Instead, they developed an intense hatred within us for the system they chose to raise us in and left us to our own devices in a drug-infested community. At the same time, they worked their fingers to the bone, many in physically draining industries, for peanuts. But it was ok because we had the Qur'an and Sunnah.

We had our halos.

Wake-Up Call

The first time I saw a dead body, I knew exactly why he was killed and had a good idea who did it. The thought of notifying the police of my suspicions never crossed my mind. "I'm way too close to this street stuff" was more prevalent.

It was the wake-up call I needed to decide the thrill of rebellion did not outweigh my desire to live. Instead, I would use my intellect to survive my circumstances and surroundings long enough to figure out how to leave them.

But if I was going to stay out of the streets, I needed something constructive to do with my free time. Staying in the house was not an option. Since I had been kicking up dust, I had no issues with procrastination or laziness. The Nothing was no match for infamy, but I knew that would change if I hung out at the house.

Hajj

The answer to my problem came when Yaseen had a visitor come to the house one day. He had on Navy Blue and white Jordans XII's, creased dark blue Guess jeans, a designer t-shirt that I didn't recognize under a Polo jacket, and a Polo hat over his reddish-brown hair. He came straight in because he was helping Umi with some groceries.

"Thank you so much, young man." Umi beamed at him as he set down the last set of bags.

"You're welcome, Sister Tasneem." The young man replied. "Is Yaseen here?"

"Masood, go get your brother," Umi told me. "Tell him... I'm sorry, young man; what's your name?"

"Hajj. Hajj Abdur-Rabbani," he said, lowering his gaze and stepping backward toward the door.

"Tell him Hajj is here," Umi said, obviously impressed by Yaseen's friend.

"YASEEN, HAJJ IS HERE!" I yelled, startling Umi. Then, I turned to Hajj and said, "I like that shirt, akh. Where'd you get it from?"

Hajj looked down at where I was pointing and let a half smile escape. "Oh, I made this. My father has a t-shirt printing shop. My brother and I do most of the designs. Me and Yaseen are heading there now."

Yaseen emerged from the back and swept Hajj out of the house, calling back to Umi, "Heading to the shop! See you later! Saalaykum!"

The shop. Sounded industrious. Sounded productive. It sounded like ... the place I needed to be.

The next day when Hajj came to pick up Yaseen, I asked if I could ride along. Hajj said his father could use all the help he could get. So I crammed into the back seat of Hajj's two-door Nissan and enjoyed the amplified version of Mobb Deep's debut album while Yaseen and Hajj smoked with the windows down. It was the first and only time I'd ride in the Nissan. Hajj opted for a more spacious Delta 88 a few weeks later, better suited for his role as the first kid from the West End Muslim community with his own car.

The Shop

When we arrived at the Thirsty Camel Sales print shop, Hajj and Yaseen put Visine in their eyes, and Hajj changed shirts. He had a few in his trunk next to the amps and woofers. The shop was located across from the infamous Magic City strip club, the Fulton County pretrial detention center, the Greyhound bus station, and the Garnett Marta Station. Remembering the times we'd walked from Five Points to Garnett to jump the rail, the block looked like a crossroads of poor decision-making. It looked like the life I was trying to save myself from.

We walked into the shop and the palpable smell of ink, paint thinner, and emulsion probably enhanced my contact high. Boxes of t-shirts were stacked to the ceiling, and one large, eight-pallet automatic silk screen machine was in motion, rotating every two seconds with one kid putting the shirts on, one taking them off, and another keeping the ink filled. Finally, the finished shirts were placed on a conveyor belt that sent the shirt under 330-degree heat to dry the ink.

It was poetry. The people running the press were my age or younger, and I recognized them as Zak's little brother Hudhayfah and the boys from the shed who weren't allowed to cross Lucille Avenue to our side of the West End.

Hajj walked me into the office, where he introduced me to his younger brother Ibrahim, a kid my age just as well dressed as Hajj. Ibrahim was a shade darker than Hajj, with curly hair that peaked from under his baseball cap, which was half on, pointing to the ceiling. Ibrahim was wholly immersed in the design he was creating on his screen, so Hajj motioned to his father and said, "Abi, this is Yaseen's brother Masood. He wants to work."

A smooth looking 6'3" with a shiny dome and sparkling dark eyes, Hajj's father walked up to me with an extended hand.

"As Salaamu Alaikum Masood. Abdullah Rabbani. Do you know how to fold shirts?"

A-B-dullah

I spent the next few hours separating by size the shirts piling up in the box at the end of the dryer, then folding them into neat dozens. The repetitious nature of folding allowed me to turn my body into a machine while my eyes observed and my mind wandered.

Brother Abdullah was fascinating because he didn't seem to be anti-anything. He found a positive slant to everything and spoke softly with an ever-present smile. But he was pro-getting money. I was amazed at his relationships with his sons and young workers. We were printing 200 dozen shirts for the upcoming Sweet Auburn festival. For my part, Brother Abdullah said he would give me one dozen shirts of my own and 20% for every shirt I sold after that. If I sold ten dozen shirts total, that would be $360 for folding and selling some shirts. I was in!

I wasn't exactly a natural salesman. On the first day of Sweet Auburn Fest, I hung very close to the stand with Ibrahim and a few others our age. I watched how they casually flirted with the girls walking by and told the men how our shirts would look better with their shoes. Everything was loud and fun. People stopped just to be a part of what appeared to be a cool situation. I was still very quiet and didn't have that kind of charm yet, in crowds.

Meanwhile, Brother Abdullah would come to the stand, load up about ten dozen shirts on his shoulder, walk off, and come back half an hour later with no shirts. Over and over and over. Finally, I decided to take my shirts and follow him.

The man was a maestro. He approached people as if he'd known them their entire lives and engaged them in conversations that sounded like a continuation.

"Hey, I've got your souvenir t-shirt right here," he'd say in an even, conversational tone walking up to a group of ladies. Without fail, they would stop, smile, and welcome his tall, dark handsomeness into the middle of their circle. Then, picking one of them to address, he'd reach for his stack of medium shirts and say, "What are you, a medium?" The woman, clearly not a medium, would blush and say, "Ooh I wish, honey! Do you have it in an extra large?"

"I sure do, and these are 100% cotton, so it'll shrink a little if you do."

Then he'd simply ask all her friends their sizes, put the shirt in their hands or over their shoulders, and when one would haggle about the price, he would take it from them, making them subconsciously fight him to keep the shirt. When men saw the group of women buying his shirt, they would stop and pull out wads of cash to impress the ladies. Brother Abdullah was a master. It was especially fascinating because he wasn't flirting with the women in a way that crossed any lines. He was happily married to Sister Khansa, a gorgeous, magnetic woman in her own right, who would crack jokes about Brother Abdullah's selling style whenever she came by the shop between shifts as a medical assistant at a nursing home. She was good as long as he put food on the table for their family of nine.

After the Sweet Auburn Fest, I settled into a routine at the shop. Bouncing between Ibrahim, Hajj, and Brother Abdullah with questions about the printing process, I worked my way from folding to cleaning and reclaiming screens to pulling shirts off the pallet onto the dryer. It took a combination of timing, concentration, and gentleness to get hundreds of shirts in a row unstuck from the pallet and onto the dryer in two seconds without smearing the design. With experience, I even learned to put the shirts on the pallets, which was the senior-most role of the automatic printing process. I could get into a zone with the abovementioned tasks and barely smelled the fumes.

I even stepped into the office occasionally and consulted Ibrahim on designs.

Road Tripping

The following few events were all HBCU classic football games around the southeast. I made it a habit to ride shotgun with Brother

Abdullah on road trips from Atlanta to Daytona, Florida, Salisbury, North Carolina, and New Orleans, Louisiana. He was the first adult male who spoke to me like a fellow man. He answered my questions about business, family, and West End history with patience and thoughtfulness. In return, he asked me questions about New Mexico and Islam because he wasn't ashamed to admit what he didn't know, and Abu had poured a lot of Islam into me.

Posted up selling t-shirts out of Abdullah's van in Galveston, TX at Spring Break 2000

Abdullah didn't make it weird and taboo when the subject of women came up. He was matter of fact.

"You're going to have a lot of choices when it comes to women. I see how they respond to you. Be careful. Running around with a bunch seems cool, but it'll hurt you more in the long run. So stick with one if you can," he told me.

How could I not take heed? This man had Sherman Helmsley's hairline yet still had ladies swooning in every city. But instead of taking

85

advantage of them, he used his powers to care for his wife and seven children.

As I got older, Brother Abdullah preferred to let me drive, giving me all the fuel I'd ever need by simply saying I was the best driver out of my crew. To prove him right, I'd stock up on Red Bull, sunflower seeds, and chewing gum, then drive straight the entire 14 hours from Atlanta to Galveston. Or ten hours to Miami or seven hours to New Orleans. He wasn't the wingman I was when he was at the wheel — he preferred to sleep on top of the shirts in the back. But that trust was the main ingredient for those long journeys.

Abdullah Abdul-Rabbani is a Giant in My Midst. He taught me what drive was. He taught me to sell to women, and the men would follow. He taught me respect didn't have to be rooted in fear or obligation. He taught me that vulnerability was not weakness.

GIANT PRINCIPLE:

It's not enough to know what you're against.
You must know what you are for.

Chapter 7:
The Ballis

Four years into the Abdul-Haqqs-move-to-Atlanta experience, the harmony we once enjoyed at home was gone. My parents' arguments over how to educate us were becoming more frequent, and the past-due notices were flowing in seemingly every day.

Too often for Umi, central heating meant a wide-open oven, and paying the electric bill meant Abu was going to go outside and rig the meter. My private school-attending, college-graduate mother and economically challenged, survivalist father were finally coming to grips with a fact my siblings and I had realized years earlier: They were about as compatible as baking soda and vinegar. In the fall of 1996, their 17-year marriage fizzled out and boiled over into a once-and-for-all divorce.

Umi gained freedom for the first time in her life.

Abu got a new, more submissive wife in weeks.

And we, the kids, got the house.

We got the house!!!

Umi moved into a one-bedroom apartment because that was all she could afford at the time, not knowing that Abu had moved in with his new wife. All of which left the Abdul-Haqq stair steps, ages 13-16, alone in a four-bedroom, one-bathroom house in the infamous West End of Atlanta, Georgia. Naturally, our house became the unofficial hangout spot for all delinquent Muslim kids within a 5-mile radius.

Oh, and I started high school.

In September 1996, I was an incoming freshman at North Atlanta High School. For most 14-year-old boys, high school represents new-found freedom. But I had just spent the bulk of my summer sans parental supervision, hanging out with a who's who of armed robbers, drug dealers, and fast girls, and making $500 to $1000 a week selling t-shirts at events around the southeast. 2875 Northside Drive was not much more than an asylum aimed to imprison me for 7 hours a day.

Because North Atlanta was the only public school in the state that offered Arabic classes, Ibrahim and many of my West End friends were at North Atlanta with me. I spent about 15 minutes of class time doing schoolwork and the other 40 minutes writing raps or thinking of ways to exploit the hoards of upper-middle-class kids that wanted to be from the hood so bad they'd overpay for the illusion.

In a few short months, we were first-year superstars at a school where most kids had known each other since elementary school. Boys that had spent all summer getting the courage to finally talk to that girl he'd been crushing on since 2nd grade were watching those girls watch us with sparkling eyes, and they didn't like it one bit. But we never backed down from any challenge and stuck together whether we were outnumbered 5 to 2 or 10 to 4. So we fought a lot and gained the respect of every person in the school in the process. I loved High School. When I went, I kept my head above water in class, but schoolwork was a side note in my first year. My newfound popularity bred confidence that must have been itching to come out for quite some time because I played up to my reputation as a hustler/fighter/ladies' man every chance I got.

All the while, the situation at home was spiraling out of control. Umi had returned briefly to restore order, and the eviction notice came just as she paid off the last of the astronomical bills Abu had left behind. The announcement that we were moving to Detroit with him shortly after that. The news didn't faze me because I knew one thing for sure: I wasn't going. If Abu thought I would leave the good thing I had helped create at North Atlanta High School, he must have been smoking something. Not to mention the little relationship I was warming up with Nikki, the bowlegged 10th grader with the long hair from my PE class...

In a sad, deathly silent house, I only told Yaseen while packing, "He got me messed up. Ain't no way in Hell I'm going to no Detroit."

And I meant it.

Run

It wasn't easy looking around the house my siblings and I had spent our first four Atlanta years in, knowing it would be my last time seeing the inside. I slumped against a window, looked outside at the broken three-foot brick wall lined one side of our elevated lawn, and remembered a high-speed chase ending our first night in the house. Little did I know then how symbolic that night would be to the crash course on city life for which I was in store.

I paced the hardwood floors and plotted my escape. I had packed my bags just like everyone else's, and my face was just as long, if not longer, than all of my siblings. I was sadder because I was about to be separated from them for the first time in my life, and only Yaseen knew about it. I didn't want Sumayyah, my second mother, or Najwa, my best friend and protege, trying to get me to stay with them. It simply would have been too hard.

Abu went to fill up on gas and get Sister Mashallah. Before leaving, he said, "Have all your bags outside and use the bathroom now. I'll be back in 15 minutes." So I slipped out the back door with nothing but the clothes I had on and made my way to 503 Atwood, the residence of my friend Jashobeam "Shobe" Balli-Nuriddin and the rest of his family. Shobe's house made the most sense because it was only three blocks away, and every family member always treated me like a brother or a son. But that still didn't help the pain of separation I felt with every step I took away from my sisters and brother. I was stubborn, though, and wasn't going to change my mind. My heart was pumping so hard that I felt my pulse in my new Adam's apple, and my ears were burning hot.

I knew this would be a pivotal decision that would shape the rest of my life, but I had no clue how.

After three knocks, I was greeted by a giant metallic smile and a "Hey Masood!" It was Shobe's younger sister Onida.

"Hey Onida, is Shobe here?" I tried to no avail to match her smile with my own.

"No, he went around the corner with Ome," Onida replied. "But you can come in. Make yourself at home."

She had no idea how literal I was taking her at that moment, but she would soon enough.

503

I never had to ask to stay at 503 Atwood with the Ballis.

Shobe's mom, who us Muslim kids in the neighborhood called Sister Imelda, never mentioned that I technically didn't belong there. A well-rounded, gray-tipped woman of Mexican and Navajo descent, Sister Imelda made it clear that I was welcome to stay before my family had traveled a significant distance up Interstate 75 North. Then, in her nasal, monotonous Chi-Town drawl, she instructed Shobe, "Find Masood some of your basketball shorts to sleep in, move the pile of clothes off Sannyasa's bed, and get some clean linens out of the back closet."

She was referring to Shobe's older brother's double bed, which still had clothes piled at least four feet atop it because he had moved out to live with his girlfriend. In one of the rare instances that Shobe obeyed his mother, he gladly made way for me.

Shobe and I wore the same shoe size, were left-handed, and his birthday was only one day before mine. So we coexisted as perfectly as two 15-year-old boys that spent 18-24 hours a day together possibly could.

One of the differences between Shobe and me was how we thought about girls. Like any teenage boy, neither Shobe nor I could get girls off our minds. But while I got giddy about the mere possibility of girls, Shobe was far more experienced and tended to objectify them in speech and action. A parade of girls from around the neighborhood would come into the house, speak to me and whoever else was there, disappear into one of the bedrooms with Shobe, and reemerge a short while later with frazzled hair and wrinkled clothing. Very few girls our age on Atwood Street didn't have an intimate relationship with Shobe.

At North Atlanta, Shobe and I had one class together, which was Spanish. Having grown up in New Mexico, a bilingual state, through 5th grade, I did well in that class. But as the end of the semester drew nearer, Shobe and I made that class less and less because it was the 6th and final period of the day. By then, Shobe and I were often already at home. Usually, we'd get to school, and he'd be looking for me to skip with him right after homeroom. But I'd hold off until at least after C lunch because I liked my English literature class and talking to my friend Khetanya at lunch. Even still, my attendance in class was becoming increasingly sporadic, as were my salats.

> The bright young Muslim straight-A student
> was acting like anything but one.

But unfortunately, I couldn't get the vicious cycle to stop spiraling out of control.

My Brother's Keeper

Not quite steady, my right hand buoyed a 3-pound firearm in the general direction of my supposed targets. Shobe looked on in stunned silence as I expelled four rounds into the crisp January night air. My shooting hand feigned recoil just before each shot fired, ensuring the bullets would fly above my fleeing targets' heads. As was often the case, I felt like I wasn't doing what I was doing, like an actor in a movie. But I wouldn't have anyone watching saying I wasn't playing my part, so I played it to the fullest.

Sure, I went in on some weed with Shobe and sold nicks and dimes to the local potheads, but I wasn't a dope boy. But Shobe was supposed to be. And as his keeper, I knew his reputation would take a hit if word spread that he didn't do anything when the middle man walked off with our re-up money, robbing him without a weapon.

Shooting that gun was an out of body experience. I felt like a witness, so no guilt overcame me. I only intended to send the message that we weren't as gravy as Shobe's actions suggested. Though he may have been a hustler and a gambler, Shobe was no gangster. Although not as experienced in the game, I had read enough Donald Goines novels and listened to enough rap music to know the best dope boys had to be all three. In my mind, I was just filling his void as any good friend would.

"How you just gonna let em take the money, Shobe? I told you I should have came with you!"

Shobe was still out of breath from his sprint back to the car from the middle of the small park where his drug deal had just gone wrong. He said nothing. I put the gun under the passenger seat of our Sprite can green 1988 Caprice Classic, and we sped off toward Atwood.

"You think you hit one of them niggas, bruh?"

Shobe had finally regained most of his breath and some of his composure.

"If I would have hit one, he woulda fell. I wasn't trying to," I replied truthfully.

Not feeling very sensitive, I asked him, "What happened, man? I thought you said you knew these dudes! What you wanna do now?"

I knew he didn't want to do anything but go home and forget about it. But I wanted him to say it, so his vulnerability was on record. I need some ammo for the next time he started one of his joke-on-Masood sessions with his new girlfriend, Bobbi, or Sannyasa. Finally, Shobe admitted he wanted to put the situation behind him, and we rode the remaining few blocks giddily, recapping the action like any pair of 15-year-olds would since we knew the scary part was over. Besides, we still had a shoebox full of cash and another pound of Kentucky's finest back at the house. The $750 we had just lost wasn't worth losing anything else for, and we chalked it up to a lesson learned.

When we got home, it was about 8 o'clock, and Sister Imelda was home with her feet up, flipping through channels and chatting with Bobbi, who had shown up while Shobe and I were out. Shobe muttered something to Sister Imelda and stomped to the bedroom. He may not have been a gangster, but he was meticulous about the books, and I knew he didn't need my help.

So I settled in next to Sister Imelda on the couch and joined in on her and Bobbi's conversation about Bobbi's upcoming trip to Trinidad with her international business class. Listening to her talk about the history of Carnival and per capita incomes in South American countries, I couldn't help but think how odd a match she and Shobe were. They had met at a North Atlanta football game back in October. Then, after our birthday party in December, they began spending more time together, usually at the house with me and the regulars at 503.

Bobbi was charming and well-liked by everyone. Not only was she a junior, but she wasn't like the ghetto bunnies I had become accustomed to seeing Shobe usher in and out of the house. Her petite 5'2 frame also went against Shobe's usual preference, and her short, layered hairstyle made her look a little older and more sophisticated than her age. She was born and raised in Atlanta, but you couldn't tell by listening to her, as she had no drawl — southern, ghetto, or otherwise, and her vocabulary rivaled mine, which was unheard of on Atwood Street.

As usual, she and I ended up monopolizing the conversation, and I didn't even notice that Sister Imelda had dozed off until Shobe stormed into the room.

"Mama!"

She jumped as she awoke. "Yes, hon?"

Shobe was livid, and I knew it could only mean one thing. "Did that m_____f*cker Sannyasa come home today?" His voice was as high-pitched as ever.

"Yes, Shobe. He just left before you guys got here. What happened?"

Shobe didn't bother answering and bolted towards the front door. I met him on the front porch, where he confirmed my suspicions.

"That nigga White Boy hit the stash, bruh. We ain't got shit!"

I knew he was going around the corner to confront his brother, so I asked if he wanted me to come.

"Naw, man, just chill here with Bobbi until I get back. I told her to come over here earlier, but I gotta handle this business."

That made it two lessons learned in one night.

Relieved I didn't have to get between the brothers, I agreed and went back inside. As I sat down, Bobbi was shaking her head.

"What's up?" I asked, almost rhetorically.

She gave me a blank look like she knew I knew exactly what she was talking about.

"He didn't even look at me once, Masood."

I knew better than to respond.

Aftermath

Come May, when my eventful first year of high school ended, Sister Imelda thanked me for being a good friend and influence on Shobe. She told me she was taking her family on vacation and that it was probably best I return to my own family. Umi was still in the one-bedroom and working multiple jobs, leaving Abu in Detroit as my only option. Umi bought me a one-way bus ticket to Detroit and promised she would get a house for all of us soon.

In 2002, Sister Imelda would become the first person in the country to lose her home because her sons sold crack there. 503 Atwood became the poster child for Fulton County District Attorney Paul Howard's plan to take crack houses from their owners, renovate them, and invite a police officer to live there rent-free. The indictments that led to the convictions and eventual seizure of 503 cited events that I was present for during my brief stay with the Ballis.

Once again, I had escaped a life and freedom-threatening situation unscathed.

Sannyasa turned his life around after serving his time, becoming an excellent family man and entrepreneur. Onida and Ayita are also raising families and climbing in their chosen fields. Unfortunately, Shobe never found a way to thrive without the luxury of fast money. As an adult, he developed a crippling gambling addiction, trying to recapture the financial freedom he enjoyed as a teenager. Bobbi and I remained close long after Shobe and I drifted apart, and I'll admit it was a little scandalous, but I had my reasons.

Sister Imelda paid the ultimate price. The loss of her home was one thing, but the stress associated with it led to her health declining until she passed away in 2009. When I talk about her, I call her my Godmother, even though there is no such concept in Islam. But you cannot convince me that Sister Imelda was not sent into my life by God during a time when I needed that motherly love most.

Shobe was my best friend for this period of my life, but **Sister Imelda** was the Giant. She's one of the people I often pray I see in heaven.

GIANT PRINCIPLE:

Be hospitable like Sister Imelda Balli, but know when to put your foot down.

Chapter 8:
April Dawn

Head jammed between my knees; I stared at the laces of my handed-down white Reebok Classics. Trying to drown out my environment, I focused on every crease my fat toes had forged into the flimsy footwear. I noticed a slight yellowing in the corner where the mid-sole met the heel. Manual bleach treatment and inadequate rinsing made the shoelaces look younger and brighter than the shoes themselves. I stared until I started resenting the shoes.

Those Classics had just carried me from a beautiful June day in Atlanta into a place where loudness went to fester. Where Atlanta's disenfranchised converged to escape bad decisions or chase new ones. A voice over the intercom announced the sold-out express Greyhound to Detroit would begin boarding in five minutes. I glanced up to see who cared about the announcement, which gave me an idea of who I would spend the next 725 miles cramped in a bus with.

A 30-something-year-old mother was rocking back and forth, trying to gather enough momentum to rise as her five children looked off with embarrassment. A stocky man in timberlands, baggy jeans, and a stocking cap holding a bag that said "City of Atlanta Department of Corrections" moved closer to the door. Then there was a solemn-looking girl with headphones on over hair that looked hard to tame. Her sad, downward-pointing eyes met mine as soon as it was her turn to be judged, and neither of us broke our gaze. We were evaluating the scene with similar apathy and diligence. Then, finally, we both went back to drowning out the world.

I boarded the bus and started scanning for the girl with sad eyes. She was in the row 21 window seat on the driver's side with the reading light on her face and her book bag and purse in the aisle seat. She moved them when I approached, then turned off the light and buried her head into a pillow when I sat down. I gathered that she was probably 18 or 19 based on certain curves in the once-over I inevitably gave her. She was primarily Black and not excited about going to Detroit. She had me by a couple of years, but we had enough in common to give me hope for a decent road trip, considering the circumstances.

She woke up when we pulled into the Chattanooga station and stared at me.

I said, "Great choice on this seat next to the bathroom, whatever your name is."

She hunched her shoulders, smiled, and replied, "My bad. I guess Rosa Parks was on to something, huh?"

I got off to stretch and grab some snacks for the road ahead.

When I returned, she said, "My name is April Dawn."

I said, "Well, that's poetic. I'm Masood."

She nodded and looked into my bag. "What did you get me?"

We connected the dots from Chattanooga to Nashville, Louisville, Cincinnati, and Detroit. She was four months pregnant and moving back to Detroit to be with her mother. I was fresh off a freshman year in high school, highlighted by running away from home, nine suspensions, and a 0.667 GPA. But I'm sure we had the most mature and diverse running conversation in the entire bus for those 725 miles.

When it was time to part ways in Detroit, it was unceremonious. We didn't try to exchange numbers or act like we were anything to each other but a literal shoulder to lean on during a brief transitional period in our lives.

April Dawn simply said, "remember me."

I replied "ok."

I smiled when I spotted Najwa running up to me outside the station. But I wouldn't have much to smile about in the months ahead. So I got into the van, and Abu said, "As Salaamu Alaikum. Welcome to Detroit, boy."

"Wa alaikum salaam," I replied dryly.

GIANT PRINCIPLE:

Stay aware of your surroundings and only invite positive energy into your space.

GIANT PRINCIPLE:

Be memorable.

Chapter 9:
Yaseen Abdul-Haqq

"That's my little big brother."

I used to cringe whenever I heard my brother say this to someone about me.

Because underneath the compliment was a coping mechanism for him feeling underaccomplished at that point in our lives. Lives that started in the same bedroom for the first 14 years could not have turned out more differently.

Yaseen was born at home to a midwife. I was born 385 days later in a hospital. So I got a birth certificate, and he didn't. Like Abu, he was great at building and fixing things with his hands. Like Umi, I was more of a thinker, reader, and writer. He was more anxious under pressure; I was more reserved.

The biggest one of those differences turned out to be the birth certificate. Because of it, I was on the grid, and Yaseen was off it. So while I was enrolling in school, getting a driver's license, or hopping on a plane to buy merchandise, Yaseen was piecing together an education in various trades by working with grown men to make ends meet.

I'm an antisocial butterfly, and Yaseen is a highly social recluse.

I don't like being around people for the sake of itself, but once I am, I go to the center of the action and act like the prom king. On the other hand, Yaseen loves people and is charming, funny, and reflective in his space. However, his spaces tend to be isolated from the rest of the world. I'm comfortable on stage under big lights. He's the king of any dim, smoke-filled room. But I didn't know exactly how different our lives and personalities were until I reunited with Yaseen in Detroit.

Yaseen took the divorce the hardest of all Umi and Abu's kids. Despite having interests and skills in common with Abu, Yaseen was always loving, sensitive, and sensing. Unfortunately, because Abu did not receive those qualities from his parents, he did not have them to give. So the hyper-nurturing empath in Umi balanced Yaseen out. Without it, he was untameable.

When I arrived in Detroit, I did not recognize my brother.

Not long after I settled into my room, a portion of the attic of Abu's three-bedroom, one-bathroom house, I heard loud pipes and even louder music outside and finally a dozen or so long, loud honks. I looked out my window and saw a big shiny red pickup truck parked in front of the house. Not knowing who it was, I kept looking at the truck to see who might get out. Finally, Sumayyah came up to the room and said, "I'm pretty sure that's Yaseen out there for you."

"For real?" I said excitedly. "That's what's up! Tell him I'm up here!"

Sumayyah raised her eyebrows. "I don't think that's gonna happen. Abu and Yaseen had a big fight, and Yaseen got kicked out."

Feeling terrible for not knowing this, I began to press Sumayyah for details.

"Like, an argument?"

Sumayyah shook her head. "No, like a *fight* fight. Yaseen and Sister Mashallah were butting heads about everything, and Abu kept taking her side until Yaseen just snapped one day. You know Abu does not play like that."

"Dang, how long has he been out of the house?" I asked, putting on my shoes by the door.

"I don't know, maybe two or three weeks. He's been driving by every morning making all kinds of noise with that stupid truck, though."

She sighed, shaking her head and smiling. "Yaseen is a mess, Masood. You need to be careful with him."

I looked at her like she was crazy and scoffed, "It's Yaseen. I think I'll be ok. Saalaykum, tell Abu I'll be back in a minute!" I slammed the door behind me.

Five minutes later, I was riding shotgun with my brother for the first time, headed southbound down Mount Elliott, a four-lane mixed residential and commercial street with stop lights every three blocks. I looked over at the speedometer, and the needle was approaching 100 miles per hour. Weaving between moving and parked cars, Yaseen was pushing that big red pickup through every intersection with all gas and no brakes.

Watching him prepare to blast through a red light without hesitation, I clutched the grip handle above the door and let out a terrified "YYYYyyyyyooooo!!!"

Yaseen looked at me like he was disappointed. "Aw, I got this. There's never any cops in this little stretch right here. You lucky my boy Akh ain't out here. We be racing down this joint."

Cops were the last thing on my mind.

Now I knew what Sumayyah meant.

Moving to Detroit was the worst thing that could have happened to Yaseen. Not only was he coping with the divorce, but he was doing it in a new city with no ID and no help. He couldn't get a job without ID and couldn't work for Abu when they were at odds. So he was 16 years old, living in an abandoned house with older Brothers who all laid carpet for a living. They sometimes hooked him up with their contractors to do handyman work. In return, he hooked up the "bando" with electricity and water with methods he'd learned from Abu. Once 'home,' they would smoke, drink Shu Wu Chi, and use a payphone up the street to try and convince young women they'd meet at the mall to let them spend the night at a house that wasn't abandoned.

When there were no carpet laying or handyman gigs, anything else that made money was on the table, from selling stolen cars to junkyards and chop shops to "executing the runout." The former explained the red truck. The latter was when they would flee from department stores at suburban malls with as many Polo shirts, shorts, and jackets as they could sprint with. I showed them how to freeze the ink tags before removing them, so the shirts didn't get stained. I may have had a little experience with executing the runout.

It saddened me to see my brother living in squalor and surrounded by danger. Technically homeless, his criminal actions were justifiable to me. I would hang out with him as much as I could, then return home to the room he got kicked out of and lose more and more respect for Abu each day. First, he let me run away without even pausing to look for me before taking off for Detroit, and now he had Yaseen in survival mode.

I'll never understand the Black American Baby Boomer tradition of abandoning sons when they needed guidance most because they dared express emotion. The "I brought you into this world, and I'll take you out" parenting style was toxic and ineffective at best and criminal at worst. Abu's penchant for corporal punishment when I was small, combined with his pride and stubbornness during this phase of our lives, put a mile-wide gulf between him and me that never fully closed. It also made me question every principle that he stood on.

So at night in my room, I would write raps, do pushups, and stew in contempt for Abu and Sister Mashallah. But I hid it well because I was not about that bando life. Besides, Sister Mashallah never did anything to me except welcome me into her home.

I didn't only take Yaseen's bedroom. I also took his job as Abu's assistant. Abu was working on an extension of a Masjid, and the subject of enrolling me in school never came up when fall rolled around, so I woke up when it was still dark outside every day, walked with Abu to Masjid Muath ibn Jabal for Fajr, then came home for a brief moment before going to work with him.

My job was to build wall frames with metal studs and hang sheet-rock on them. It was boring, and the site was not fully enclosed as the Michigan winter came, so it was freezing cold. But I got into a groove with my measurements and figured out the most efficient ways to screw those 3/4 inch thick sheetrock on those studs. Abu was used to having Yaseen as a helper, and Yaseen could do everything. I could sense Abu's frustration with my lack of carpentry skills outside my one specialty, so I was careful not to make many mistakes.

As winter wore on, my siblings and I began to see the light at the end of the tunnel. Umi married Abu Shaka Abdush-Shakur, whom I knew and respected. They invited Sumayyah, Yaseen, Najwa, and me back to Atlanta to live in Abu Shaka's house, only one block from our first home. It was a more spacious house closer to the park, the Masjid, and Shobe's place, so I was excited. We were to return shortly after my 16th birthday.

Until I received that news, I had been content deferring my pay from Abu. I would overhear the Bengali man in charge making excuses to Abu, and I heard Abu accepting the excuses as fact. But once I knew I would leave soon, I began to pressure Abu about my money. My brother was homeless a few blocks away, so I didn't put anything past Abu at this point. His simply not paying me was a possible outcome in my mind. I had earned nearly $2,500 and could picture the hero's return it, and my new muscles would afford me when I got back to Atlanta.

One late November morning drive to pick up some "yardbird" — Abu's word for curry fried chicken — not long after hearing the Bengali man explain to Abu why he had to pay him a fraction of what he owed yet again, I asked him, "Why do you keep letting that man chump you off?"

"You better watch who you're talking to, boy." Abu scowled and looked me up and down before continuing. "This is a Masjid. Our real reward for this job is in the aakhira (hereafter) anyway."

"Yeah, well, I need my money before the aakhira," I said, looking out the front passenger window, then to my father, who had his left hand on the wheel and a free right fist forming.

"You gonna punch me and kick me out the house too? I know that's your MO."

Abu had heard enough and began to pull the van over. But if he was about to punch me with that right fist, I wasn't going to sit there and wait for it. So I rushed him.

I got beat up by my father's right fist in the passenger seat of a moving van that day. But I got some licks in, more for Yaseen than for myself. I had it coming because Abu was a lot of things, but he was not a liar or a thief. I would have gotten paid. Abu kicked me out of the van, putting a two-mile walk through the dirty Detroit snow between me and home. When I arrived, I was greeted by a laughing Sister Mashallah, whose step aside let me know I wasn't kicked out of the house. Abu must not have felt I could survive on my own.

Later that night, I got a knock on my door. When I opened the door, Abu handed me an envelope, rubbed the top of my head vigorously, shoved my head away from him at the end, and walked off. I peeked inside the envelope and saw 30 crisp $100 bills.

On our last weekend in Detroit, I took Yaseen and his entire car-pet-laying crew to Niki's, a Greek pizza joint downtown. I also bought some black Air Maxes and a few pieces to match. I didn't want to return to Atlanta, still wearing Sannyasa's hand-me-downs. Also, I hadn't heard from any of my friends in Atlanta except Khetanya and Bobbi the entire time I was in Detroit, so I needed to remind everyone who I was.

A-Town Bound

Returning to Atlanta in mid-December during winter break gave us time to settle in before returning to school. Sumayyah and Najwa happily bunked in their new room and got to know Abu Shaka. I played nice at home while getting back in the mix on Atwood and at the shop.

Now 17 years old, the Yaseen who returned to Atlanta refused to respect anyone solely based on age or status. After spending that time fending for himself in the streets of Detroit, he was not one to be controlled or spoken to like a child. So he got kicked out of his basement room before the New Year after clashing with his new stepfather. So I moved into the basement while he married and moved into an apartment down the street from Abu Shaka's house. He spent the next few years forming Royal Brothers, a street vending booth that sold mix CDs and apparel at kiosks around the city, and developed a good feel for business in the process.

Aftermath

After decades of going back and forth with the State of Texas, Yaseen finally got his birth certificate in 2017, and his life changed overnight.

With the help of his wife, Thoko (Toe-koe), he saw the need for affordable short-distance transportation in Atlanta. So he formed Royal Motorsports, which specialized in selling and repairing scooters and other small-engine vehicles.

The company grew, with Thoko running the marketing and sales between traveling Nurse calls. Money was coming in, and they lived comfortably, but both felt the strain from the daily grind of entrepreneurship in a big city. Yaseen had proven to himself that he could be successful on the grid, but he wanted back off.

So Thoko pushed him.

They sold their house and bought 20 acres of isolated, sage-covered land in Northern New Mexico. Sage is one of the world's most resilient crops, indicating that the soil was not very fertile. But Yaseen and Thoko were all in.

They drilled a well, figured out how to set up a solar power grid, and began making a home. Yaseen and Thoko live off the land and run Sage Garden Farms with little overhead. They grow their crops, raise chickens and sell the sage in small bundles along with tips on moving off-grid to their growing following of over 125,000 people who aspire to be free from the matrix.

This is what modern nation-building looks like. Several world-changing events hit Yaseen and forced him to rebuild his life. As a result, he has built one of the most impressive shows of human strength, resilience, and ingenuity I have ever witnessed.

My Big Brother and his wife are Black History in the Making.
They are Giants in Our Midst.

GIANT PRINCIPLE:

Never Quit. Regardless of the hand
you are dealt, everyone has royal potential.
Plan and persevere. New frontiers await!

Chapter 10:
Ebro Rabbani

Our Shining Prince

On Friday, September 25, 1998, I was on Atwood Street when three of my older peers invited me to participate in a "sweet lick." A sweet lick is a robbery that is like taking candy from a baby. They said I had to drive them to a location and let them do the rest. I had access to weapons and a vehicle, sure. But being a wheelman for some guys looking to take something from someone not much different from me was not my thing.

Besides, it was a humid extended summer night in the West End, and there were plenty of distractions to take my mind off the fact that I was just casually offered an opportunity to commit a class A felony.

I declined without pause and forgot about it.

An hour or so later, several gunshots rang out. Again, this was par for the course in the hood. But a trained ear listens for patterns to determine the seriousness of the shots. Sometimes semi-automatic handguns were let off pretty rapidly in celebration or to show off. You might hear a single blast, which could be a kill shot or a warning. Neither of these patterns is usually a threat to the community at large.

This time though, there were several shots from one handgun — in no particular rhythm — followed by a more extended, louder response from a larger caliber gun, then more shots from the first gun. This meant it was a shootout.

The proximity of the shots put everyone on Atwood on edge because a shootout meant desperate men with guns were on the move. Also, the closer the shots, the more likely it was that anyone hit was someone you knew.

Nervous energy spread up and down the block, but we didn't go inside. News traveled quickly in the hood, and we knew if we waited long enough, someone would come down the street with a report. We didn't have to wait long.

Some of the dope boys from nearby Hopkins Street rolled through ten minutes later to check on us, see if we were ok, and offer *condolences*.

They mentioned something about the car wash five blocks away and rolled off before telling us what they meant. So a group of us made a quick jog in that direction and arrived on the scene just as the police were taping off the area surrounding the self-service car wash.

Inside one of the stalls was a black 1985 Oldsmobile Delta 88 with the driver's side door open.

A pair of black Jordan IVs could be seen under the door, pointed toward the sky, lifeless, with a puddle of blood pooling around the victim's legs.

We knew immediately.

It was Hajj Abdur-Rabbani.

By 16, I was no stranger to homicide. From the first body I'd seen at 14 to the countless drug dealers and armed robbers who had dropped afterward, I had become numb to the idea of guys I'd had conversations with and knew personal details about simply no longer existing.

My friends and I had become so desensitized to it when certain shootings happened, and the news came down about who the victim was, we would glance at each other, then race to his known stash spots to claim whatever bankrolls, drug stashes or weapons they'd left behind.

Death was a sport to us.

It was easy to 'otherize' non-Muslims playing a deadly game and losing.

Until September 25, 1998, it was never one of *us* when someone in the hood died.

I must have fainted or blacked out. I rose from one knee and saw my friends edging closer to the car, wanting to see Hajj. A crowd was forming, and people I knew and loved were sobbing and confirming that 18-year-old Hajj — our shining, good-mannered prince — fresh off his high school graduation and Clark Atlanta University bound, had lost his life.

And I knew it was because he accepted a mission that I had declined.

Chosen Brothers

I spent most of that night crying and trying to make sense of the world I was a part of, realizing for the first time that becoming a drug dealer, murderer or going to prison wasn't the worst-case scenario.

For the first time, my halo flickered.

The following day, I woke up and began walking with no particular destination. I allowed my mind to drift as my legs carried me south onto Holderness Street and then east onto Egleston Street. I was almost halfway there when I realized I was heading to the Rabbani's house. I shuddered at the thought of how Hajj's death must affect Ibrahim.

Ibrahim, or Ebro as we affectionately called him, and I had grown close during all those late nights in the shop and road trips. We had stood back to back in fights against much larger groups in school and held our own. We were only three months apart in age and shared a fondness for Brother Abdullah, getting fresh and making money, among other things. But Hajj was Ebro's best friend and hero.

Hajj's dream to start a clothing line was all he talked about and worked toward. Ebro was far from shy, but he wasn't nearly as cerebral or gregarious as Hajj was and preferred to make designs, while Hajj focused on big-picture business planning.

Hajj's drive and strategic mind, combined with Ebro's boldness, creativity, and those Rabbani good looks, left no doubt they would be an extremely successful tandem and take over the fashion world.

It just wasn't meant to be.

As I got halfway down Egleston street, I noticed a kid in a white and royal blue Polo shirt, a blue L.A. Dodgers hat pointed up and to the left, baggy khaki shorts, and white and blue Jordan IVs sauntering toward me, kicking a rock with his hands in his pockets. It was Ebro.

When he approached, his face was puffier than usual, and his eyes were red but dry. Not knowing what to say to a guy whose brother had been killed only hours earlier, I hugged him with both arms. He hugged me back, pulling me closer, and we stood there embracing for what seemed like an eternity for two kids who usually had a handshake in between our brief bro hugs.

I turned in the direction he had been heading, back toward Holderness, and we walked the neighborhood together, covering block after block, reminiscing on Hajj's brief yet impactful life.

For me, Hajj was a chess partner, fellow fisticuffs fan (we'd had a few rumbles together, too), style guide, and occasional ride to work. For Ebro, he was everything.

Ebro held a picture of Hajj and glanced at it occasionally. Finally, we stopped and sat on a short wall where he confessed, "I never saw him in my dreams."

I asked what he meant.

Ebro exhaled, looked at the ground, shook his head, and replied, "All my life, I saw myself getting millions and having a family and building a big house right here in the West. But bro was never in my dreams. It's like Allah was trying to tell me he wasn't part of my future."

He paused again, gathered himself as if to prevent himself from crying, and continued, "Now I gotta do it big enough for both of us." I put my arm around him and replied, "You always have a brother in me, bro."

Rabbani World

After Hajj's funeral, Ebro called a meeting. Present were myself, brothers Ahmad and Fakeer Abdullah, who went to North Atlanta High school with us, and Zak's brother Hudhayfah. We gathered around the Abdur-Rabbani's attic-turned-bedroom in their home on West End Place, where Ebro presented us with some of Hajj's sketches and business plans. He declared he wanted to carry out Hajj's dream of starting a clothing line. But, he pressed, he needed our help to do so.

By this point, we had extensive experience making and selling t-shirts together and had even begun hustling anything else of value that we could get our hands on at the suburban magnet school. So Ebro proposed that we form a clothing company named Rabbani in honor of Hajj.

We loved the idea but balked at the name.

We argued that Ebro was a Rabbani, and it would appear that we all just worked for him. Finally, after some discussion, we arrived at the name R. World Shirt Company.

The idea behind R. World was to compliment what was already hot in the fashion game with our distinct, colorful shirt designs. In those days, fleece, nylon, velour, and jean suits were all the rage, but we peeped a weakness in the shirt selection.

Many simply threw a white t-shirt under their jacket and called it an outfit. But, thanks to Ebro and my unauthorized same-day jaunts to Canal Street in Manhattan, we were already fashion trendsetters at school. So incorporating our custom-designed shirts into our Sean John, Iceberg, Cybertek, Polo, Maurice Malone, Guess, Eddie Bauer Ebtek, Eckó, and Enyce ensembles was easy. We'd have matching new shirts ready on new Jordan or Air Max colorway release dates. All it took was for us to each rock a different color scheme to school on the release day to sell five dozen shirts the day after. After repeating this cycle enough times and knocking down enough doors, we landed the contract for Atlanta Public Schools' junior and senior class shirts for 1999 and 2000.

In a nod to our Islamic background, we also created the Calligraphy Collection, a signature collection of colored t-shirts which featured some of the 99 Names of Allah written in beautiful Arabic scripts.

That way, we could simultaneously appease our parents and community elders and raise more money at Muslim conventions. It was a true win-win.

Ebro and I, surrounded by the crew on Holderness Street in 2002

Come graduation time, leaving high school was bittersweet. If we were to continue, we'd have to leave a clear blue ocean without competition for a bloody red one in the public sector. But we embraced that challenge. As a result, everyone except Ahmad decided to forego college to build R. World into a nationally recognized brand.

'A' Business Lesson

Our first design after leaving school was not Ebro's most creative one. It was a simple lowercase letter 'a' on a Ragland, or baseball T. The colors on the sleeve and collar matched the colors on the 'a.' If you've seen a photo of Atlanta Braves legend Hank Aaron in a Braves uniform, you've seen the design. Stores like The Athlete's Foot, Lids, Foot Locker and Fame had been selling the vintage Braves 'a' hats for years but with little to no accompanying apparel. Ebro saw an opportunity to swoop in and fill a void, so he went to work.

The beauty of R. World was that we were our target demographic. We were a bunch of determined, admired, handsome young men with a street edge. We got into more than our share of trouble throughout high school, but we did it looking fresh. Ebro won Most Attractive in his senior yearbook and was runner-up for best dressed. I got kicked out of North Atlanta after ninth grade for excessive fighting and cutting class, but recovered and ended up at Washington High, where I would pop my trunk, and people swarmed because they knew I always had some kind of hot new fashion in there.

We were the tastemakers.

We hit the streets of Atlanta the same way we used to hit the halls in high school — each of us in a different color shirt, with a hat and shoes to match. We'd split into pairs and knock on every urban clothing store's door within a 20-mile radius of downtown Atlanta, dressed how we wanted them to wrap their mannequins.

The Lowman Wins

Because of the charm-dependent, cold-selling nature of moving merchandise at beach and tailgate parties, we thought we had mastered the art of the sale. But the first six weeks of pitching our A shirts were a sobering experience.

No one bit, not the Nigerians, the Senegalese, the Koreans, the Chinese, or the white store owners. Each time we'd pitch the A shirts, we got a variation of "That's cute, but these hats barely even sell. So why would the shirts sell?"

They didn't get it. The hats didn't sell *because* they didn't have the shirts.

Just as things were starting to look bleak enough to question whether we had made the right choice by skipping college, Ebro made a breakthrough. He landed a meeting with the owner of a handful of The Athlete's Foot apparel stores, including the busiest one in the city, located at Underground Atlanta.

His name was Isom Lowman, and he was a young Black man, maybe 12 years older than us. Isom was tall and had a smooth, southern charm in conducting business. In just a few short years, he had come out of nowhere to challenge Atlanta hip-hop apparel icon Walter Strauss for the downtown Atlanta sneaker sales crown.

Isom started by franchising The Athlete's Foot name in locations across the Atlanta metro area. By the time Ebro landed the meeting with him, Isom had also built a superstore under his brand, FAME, to act as a competitor to his Athlete's Foot at Underground Atlanta. But, of course, guys his age weren't making those kinds of moves back then, so Isom stood out among impressive Black businesspeople in the city.

I was impressed by boardroom Ebro because many of the terms of the deal that he spat out at Isom and countered were a foreign language to me at the time. But he had studied Hajj's notes well.

As soon as Ebro finished pitching Isom the 'A' shirts, Isom was all-in. He agreed to try out 50 dozen shirts in five colors on a Net-60 consignment deal at $100 per dozen. Of course, we had about $5.50 invested in every shirt, so 600 shirts at $8.33 per shirt wasn't a huge deal. But still, we had our first client, and he was in a position to put R. World on the map.

Isom made R. World a priority, setting up window displays that looked just like we did when we pitched the 'A' shirts in Isom's office — with the hat, colorful Dickies shorts, and shoes to match. The Athlete's Foot blew through the first order in two weeks and re-upped with a more substantial amount for both The Athlete's Foot and FAME. That's when 'A' shirts and hats started flooding the city.

The Nigerian, Senegalese, Korean, Chinese, and white vendors who scoffed at the 'A' shirts just weeks before were now blowing us up for them. We were happy to accommodate, but now our cost was closer to $3 and their price was $11 per shirt.

Faces and Voices

I remained Ebro's most trusted confidante when the lights shut off. As the group's writer, I wrote all copy for R. World, including flyers, websites, sales brochures, commercial scripts, and company manuals. To capture the essence of R. World in words, Ebro and I had deep conversations about the company's purpose, mission, and vision, three things we didn't always agree on. If Ebro was the company's heart and face, Fakeer and Ahmad were two halves of its brain, and I was its voice. As the voice, my responsibility included telling Ebro when he was straying from the vision he shared with me on September 26, 1998.

Days that shall live in infamy

On September 11, 2001, we watched the news in awe from our brand new office with the rest of the world as the twin towers collapsed. Ebro and I had flown into LaGuardia airport several times to go shopping on Canal Street. The terrifying visual of someone hijacking and steering the plane into one of the skyscrapers was not hard to conjure. A few of our bank accounts were frozen in 9/11's aftermath, thanks to some guys named Masood, Rabbani, and Abdullah, who had dealings with Osama bin Laden. It was a ridiculous reaction for the government to take on its citizens after some foreigners committed a heinous act. So we had to carry a lot of cash around for a while, which was a little dangerous where we lived. It was inconvenient but far from the worst thing that happened to us that month.

On October 3, 2001, a passenger on a Greyhound bus heading from Chicago to Orlando took a boxcutter and slit the driver's throat while driving, killing him. The bus swerved and landed on the side of I-75 south in a rural part of Tennessee. Six passengers died, and a seventh was rushed to Vanderbilt Hospital with massive injuries to her chest cavity.

The victim's name? Khansa Abdur-Rabbani.

Ebro's mom had been heading back to Atlanta after visiting her family in Ohio. So, once again, we rallied around the Rabbani family in the wake of tragedy — beelining to Nashville to be with them in hopes of receiving better news than we did just three short years and one week earlier.

Ebro was despondent the entire time. He was numb.

Day after day, we'd gather in the waiting room and wait. The doctors would update us on Umi Khansa's condition, which sounded dire and painful.

After a few days, Brother Abdullah sent his children and us friends home to Atlanta. Then, on October 9, Ebro, his brother Hudhaifa and his sisters Halimah, Khatiymah, and Asantewaa were rocked by the news that Sister Khansa was gone.

Losing Religion

He never told me this, but it felt like Ebro lost faith that day. Like at first, he thought losing Hajj was unfortunate, but now it felt like Allah was actively targeting him and his family. I never saw the puffy face or lost, red eyes that were ever present when Hajj died. In their place was steely-eyed determination and resolve. Instead, he became obsessive - maniacal even - about working. He borrowed personality traits from Al Pacino's Scarface and Michael Corleone characters and took business cues from hip-hop mogul Master P. He demanded respect from allies, competitors, and customers and perfection from every R. World employee. He wanted R. World to be bigger than life and thought micromanaging was the way to achieve it.

When the insurance and lawsuit settlements from the Greyhound crash came, Ebro used his share to invest even more money into R. World. The size of his stake grew to make him the undisputed boss of all bosses. In the months to come, Ebro took no days off. Not for therapy, not for vacation, or even a quick breather. His moves to position R. World atop the hip-hop clothing landscape solidified Ebro as one to watch on the Atlanta Business scene while the rest of us happily propped him up behind the curtains. His bold, childlike, artistic nature suffered from the growing list of responsibilities as CEO of a rapidly expanding company, but it did not die.

Creative Ebro and CEO Ebro were two different people, but he could flip the switch with a little effort. It was as if Hajj lived inside of him and came out when it was time to run meetings, negotiate deals or forge a path forward for R. World. As we experienced more success, saw more money, and employed more people, Ebro became less accustomed to being told no, stop or don't. That meant it was even more critical that I did, even if it meant him getting upset at me. No matter how friendly we were or were not, I would always be his brother.

The Image of Success

In the summer of 2002, Ebro and I decided to go to the most prominent apparel expo in the world, the Magic Show in Las Vegas. The Magic

Show was where manufacturers, wholesalers, and retailers of clothes could all be under the same roof simultaneously, exchanging information and ideas and forming alliances.

We spent our days in Vegas soaking up knowledge about the industry we were trying to dominate. Then, at night we mapped out what would become the new standard operating procedures for the company. First, we agreed to lean on our street credibility to expand our brand and media presence. We would do so by projecting a larger-than-life image of success. Our target demographic was not interested in helping someone too much like themselves come up but loved to support winners.

Outside of the usual tasks around the shop that everyone shared and writing copy, my job was to control product placement and marketing. And my special project was to Executive Produce a documentary that used our everyday activities to educate our audience about business and solidify us as kings of Atlanta hip-hop fashion.

We decided to make our deliveries to the growing list of stores around the southeast in audacious-looking Suburbans, Denalis, and Escalades wrapped in R. World designs and sitting on 24-inch chrome wheels. The trucks would serve as mobile billboards as our shirts were delivered. And the driver would not just be a delivery guy but a salesman. So when a store owner or manager received their R. World merchandise, they would also be shown a book of our latest designs and invited to add to their order instantly with shirts already in the truck.

We left Vegas with manufacturing connections, a preview of what would come in the fashion game next spring, and even bigger dreams than we'd started. We'd be back within three years with one of the biggest, livest booths in the entire Magic Show.

Town Business

We came home to a cease-and-desist order from the Braves for using the old logo. The Braves said they would sue R. World for copyright infringement if we did not stop using their old logo. Ebro took it as a compliment that the Braves knew his work. He also took it as a challenge.

Neither the word "cease" nor "desist" were in Ebro's vocabulary.

He doubled down and bet that R. World would be clear if we changed the lowercase 'A' to a barely different font with the word TOWN running down the now squared-off tail. He was right. The 'A' shirts became A-Town shirts, and it was up from that point forward.

Damn!

If you grew up in Atlanta in the early 1990s, you felt a kindred spirit with smooth, slick-talking cats like Big Gipp from Goodie Mob and Big Boi from Outkast — there seemed to be similar characters in every hood. But Atlanta hip hop was developing into much more than a local flavor. It was becoming mainstream. Major media outlets consistently named Gipp and Big Boi's group mates André 3000 and Ceelo Green as versatile musical geniuses and international superstars. And the next generation was right behind them.

Our fellow Westside of Atlanta resident T.I.'s rise to fame was particularly interesting to me because he looked and sounded like he could be one of us — pretty, fresh, country as hell, somewhat small, but known to fight. And like a proper young ATLien, his hat was never entirely on his head. So I guess it was a Westside thing. I remember watching his "24's" video and shaking my head because the only thing missing was an A-Town shirt.

We were sitting on a hot brand in a place and time where our culture was shaping pop culture worldwide. Given my role, I felt a personal responsibility to leverage this into exponential growth for R. World.

I started showing up at video shoots for artists around the city. I was on the set for Ying Yang Twins, Young Jeezy, and Usher videos. It felt like I was making progress after meeting a few of the artists and giving some of them shirts. But when the videos would air, the A-Town shirts would be nowhere to be found. After a while, I gave up on the artists and decided to go after the entourages, especially the stylists.

Everything changed when I met a nerdy-looking producer named Harvey "DJ Speedy" Miller. Speedy was Big Gipp's producer. After meeting at a video shoot, Speedy invited me to Gipp's house. I pulled up to the property in a quaint neighborhood near Greenbriar Mall and saw Gipp leaning on a pearl white Cadillac Deville identical to mine, saying goodbye to his ex-wife and fellow artist Joi. I knew all about them and their relationship but had to play it off.

"Hey… what up, Gipp? Uh… Speedy said to come through… uh…he here?"

Gipp smiled, flashing a platinum grill, and said in his signature deep-voiced drawl, "Yeah, he should be through them doors right there and up them steps."

Once inside, I met most of the Dungeon and Attic crews, a collection of some of the most iconic and hottest artists in the world at the time. I passed out shirts to people whose lyrics I knew like the back of my hand but still actively listened when they introduced themselves as if I had no clue. I worked the entire room and eventually felt like I belonged in it.

A few weeks later, the video for the hottest song in the country came out. It was called Damn! by YoungBloodZ ft. Lil Jon, but it may as well have been an R. World commercial.

Sean Paul, the star of the Attic Crew's YoungBloodZ, was wearing an A-Town shirt in several scenes throughout the video and even said "It's A-TOWN" three times at the beginning of the song as if to sound out how to pronounce our city's nickname and the name of our shirts.

Sean Paul became a friend of mine and would chirp me on my Nextel before any video shoot. Check out the videos for Damn! 'Or I Smoke, I Drank' with Roy Jones Jr. to see how hard he was repping for R. World.

In 2003, the video for a Billboard number 1 song immediately went into constant rotation on MTV, BET, and VH1 several times a day worldwide. When the video for 'Damn!' aired for the first time, our cellphones and office phones blew up with congratulations and, more importantly, orders.

R. World was in.

Stop Snitch'n

While I was working the Atlanta rap scene, Ebro followed up on a connection he had made with Dipset rappers Cam'ron and Juelz Santana at the Magic Show. Of course, we had been fielding custom orders for t-shirts since high school, and rappers were our peers, so Dipset's small custom order didn't move the needle much.

Their request was for tall white t-shirts with a classic red STOP sign, except they wanted the sign riddled with bullet holes and the word "Snitch'n" scribbled underneath the word STOP in a graffiti-like font. Ebro knocked the design out in a day, sent the artwork to the print team, and shipped the shirts shortly after Vegas.

I was not expecting what happened next.

In 2004, Cam'ron was not just another rapper. With his knack for eye-popping outfits and audacious punchlines, Cam'ron was a rising cultural icon in the world's fashion capital. The Harlem-born MC and his crew got our Stop Snitch'n shirts and rocked them all over New York and in videos. After a while, Dipset fans from up and down the east coast started to demand the Stop Snitch'n shirts.

I opposed mass-producing Stop Snitch'n shirts as an official R. World line. Ebro and I often talked about building R. World into a multinational brand name, and I didn't see Stop Snitch'n as a path to becoming one. Our executive team meetings turned into debates about how "hood" we were willing to allow our brand to become in the name of building buzz and capital. Ebro pointed to the local and mainstream success of T.I. and the infamous-turned-famous drug cartel, the Black Mafia Family, as examples of hood being the new chic. Rarely did a majority of us oppose Ebro at this point, so despite my best efforts, Stop Snitch'n shirts went into mass production and became R. World's second hit concept.

At this time, I learned just how accurate the axiom "controversy sells" really was.

Like the A-Town shirts, a Stop Snitch'n shirt elicited a reaction when people first laid eyes on it. And they both had the signature rectangular black and white R. World patch on the bottom right on the front of the shirt. But that's where the similarities ended.

The reaction to the A-Town shirts was always positive — something about the bright colors or city pride.

But Stop Snitch'n shirts elicited things like F the police shouts and icy glares from the police themselves. Moreover, it labeled the person wearing the shirt as anti-establishment and sometimes made them a target.

Because they made their debut in the Northeast, that's where most of our early Stop Snitch'n clientele came from. Boutique urban hip-hop clothing stores across New York City, Philadelphia, Baltimore, and D.C. all loved the Stop Snitch'n shirts. They ordered them in much larger quantities than their contemporaries in the Southeast had been ordering A-Town shirts. I couldn't help but reflect on how times had changed. Instead of flying into New York to buy clothes to sell at school, we were shipping clothes to New York that would get kids kicked out of school.

In 2004, fresh off one of the greatest college basketball seasons of all time, Denver Nuggets rookie Carmelo Anthony appeared in a documentary video called 'Stop Snitching!' In the video, Anthony was simply hanging out in his old neighborhood in Baltimore, giggling while an older man rambled about not snitching to the police. Of course, it was silly and ill-advised for the newly minted superstar, but the backlash was anything but laughable. Suddenly news outlets from Baltimore to Denver and everywhere in between were discussing hood crime culture and the pros and cons of snitching.

Spoiler alert: there were no cons.

It wasn't long before R. World became part of the national discussion as a leading wholesaler of Stop Snitch'n shirts.

As spokesman, this meant it was my time to shine.

Nationally syndicated radio and tv shows invited me to debate with trained shock jocks and law enforcement officials. On TV, I always made a point to play up every hood stereotype, draping one of our designs in size XXL over my 5'11, 155-pound frame and asking everyone in the company for their iced-out chains. I'd flip my hat up and to the left, then calmly disassemble every argument they spit out there, despite my personal beliefs on the shirts.

After word got out that I was holding my own in debates, one TV station in Denver went as far as to bring the mother of a murdered witness on air. With a gotcha look on his face, the host asked me, "What would you say to this mother who lost her child to violence when he gathered the courage to testify against a violent criminal?"

"I would say I'm sorry for your loss, ma'am."

"Thank you." The mother replied.

"Your son made a deal with the police to testify in court?" I asked her.

"Yes."

"Knowing what you know now about how the police protected your son, would you recommend other mothers allow their sons to do the same?" I asked quietly.

"No, I wouldn't," came her reply.

"That's all we're saying, ma'am."

Shifting my attention back to the shocked host, I continued.

"The authorities have the technology to track a fly from the moon if they want. But they don't truly care about solving violent crime in the hood unless we, the citizens, risk our lives to gift-wrap the entire case for them. I lost countless friends to murder, and there was a ton of evidence and several witnesses each time. But the cases are unsolved to this day."

The host replied, "Don't you think it's your civic duty to help the police remove violent criminals who murdered your friends off the street?"

I replied, "Our company, R. World Shirt Company, is owned entirely by Black men under the age of 25, and we employ over 50 people — many of whom would be in the streets if not for the opportunity R. World provides them. The amount of work that it takes to build and run a company of this scale is significant. But you wanna know who never shows up to ask if they can help us print or fold a shirt? The police. They don't help us do our jobs, so why should we risk our lives to help them do theirs?" I smiled a smile that matched the diamonds dancing on my borrowed pendants.

"Interesting perspective." The host responded. "We're going to go to break. Next up, sports!"

Producers would always rave about my performance once we were off the air and tell me I had a future as an attorney. I didn't know at the time that was another way of saying I was a schmuck. So I just shrugged it off and told them where they could send the footage. I needed it for our documentary.

The Talk

R. World checked off every single item on the list Ebro and I had created in 2002. By the time the 2005 summer Magic Show rolled around, we had a rapidly growing list of client stores across the Southeast and the Atlantic coast and a national buzz.

We showed up in Vegas with 12 of our best salespeople, trained to make our booth — one of the largest urban booth spaces outside of industry titans Sean Jean, Ecko, and South Pole — the most memorable. Our documentary, 'I'mma Show You How to Hustle,' was just completed and sure to add a layer of authenticity with its jarring depictions of life in the hood projecting from the screens at the front of our booth. Finally, we had one tricked-out box truck with flat screens on every inside wall and our faces and logo on every outside wall parked outside the convention center during the day and patrolling the Las Vegas strip garnering stares from tourists from all over the planet at night. We had created success to the tune of around $10 million and made it look like $100 million.

If we played our cards right, we thought a million dollars in orders and a much more lucrative licensing deal were within the realm of possibility. Having been there before, I took it upon myself to take the lead on setting up the booth, which meant unloading everything from the box truck at the docks by 7 AM.

So when Ebro, Hudhayfah, Ahmad, Fakeer, and other team members approached me about going out to the casinos our first night in Vegas, I declined, telling them I had some writing I needed to get done.

Ebro frowned.

"It's starting to feel like you ain't really all the way down with the team no more, Suede." That was my nickname.

Ahmad made a face that said he agreed.

I looked at Fakeer and Hudhayfah and could tell they wanted to hear my response.

"I'm down for the work. But I ain't come here to trick off. Y'all can have that," I said.

"But you be the main one tricking off in the A, though! Every time we cliqued up, Suede out with Suki. Suede with the rappers. Suede ain't nowhere to be found! Now we out here, and you wanna stay in the room??"

Ebro's voice was rising.

"I don't drink, I don't smoke, and I don't gamble. So why the hell would I be in a casino all night when we have to set up the booth first thing in the morning??"

My voice met Ebro's where his was.

Ahmad chimed in. "It's not just the casino. You're always on a solo mission. You're always arguing about the direction of the company. You still have the hotel job. You show up when the cameras are rolling, but you're not fully committed." Ahmad was the company's president and was always in lockstep with Ebro.

I felt my ears getting hot and my chest cavity tightening. This was obviously an intervention that they had been discussing for some time.

I replied, "My thing is, we started out with the Calligraphy Collection. At what point did we stop being a Muslim company? I kick it with rappers and do the club thing because I'm doing my job. It's not like y'all give me a budget to get these shirts all over national tv. Y'all be wanting to have R. World night at the strip club just because… flaunting your sins. Hell yeah, I'd rather be ducked off with Suki!"

Fakeer stepped in, seeing it was getting heated. He put his hand on Ebro's chest and said, "Let's go, bruh. Let him stay." He made a gesture that said, "it's cool," to me as they made their way to the door.

"Try to get back to your $39 luxury Las Vegas hotel room at a decent time so we can set up in the morning, Ahmad!" I called after them while the door was shutting, reminding them how my outside life benefited the company.

The next morning I woke up for Fajr and took three of our younger employees down to the convention center loading dock to start setting up the R. World booth while the rest of the executive team was knocked out.

TheiR World

This was the beginning of the end of my time at R. World. In the following months, Ebro demoted Ahmad from the role of President and appointed his older brother, recently released from prison, to the role. Under their leadership, R. World moved into a large retail building downtown, stuck a huge billboard on top of it, and began making shirts and shoes that promoted the drug culture unabashedly.

I left the company on bad terms, with Ebro's brother alleging that I was stealing because of the couple of dozen shirts I'd learned to keep in my trunk, so I was video shoot ready when artists chirped me. During the ordeal, I experienced my first death threat, lost my car, and lost contact with every significant male relationship I had built since I was 12. I was 24.

R. World only lasted about another six months after I left. The rising overhead due to the new fast and loose management style combined with the deterioration of Ebro's support system proved too difficult for the company to overcome.

Square One

After abruptly losing my R. World income and transportation, I scraped around for a few months before moving out of my townhouse back to the 4th Ward apartment that I had been subleasing for two years. I got a job at a Hampton Inn as a night auditor and put myself on a strict financial diet, walking or biking a mile and a half each way to work every night. The job was quiet and allowed me to read and work out like never before. I was still 155 pounds on my 25th birthday and vowed to be 185 by my 26th. I hit my weight target, bought a new 5-speed Mustang in my favorite shade of blue, and enrolled in college for the first time, choosing an international business major.

One night before work, my phone rang. An unsaved number I recognized was displayed on my caller ID.

"Hello?" I answered slowly.

"Saalaykum Suede."

"Who dis?" I asked, knowing the answer.

"It's your brother."

…

"Ebro, nigga! Come holla at me. I'm outside."

Outside? I thought, walking slowly to the window at the end of my apartment's second-floor hallway, where there was a window to the street.

"Hello?" Ebro asked.

"Uh … yeah … here I come. What you whipping?"

"I'm out here in the Escalade," Ebro replied. I saw it to my right in front of my Mustang.

I went back into the apartment to put a shirt on over my tank top, then stopped, mind racing.

Nah, he's about to see these gains.

But what is he on?

Is this hostile?

I'm not taking any chances.

I grabbed my .45 caliber P95 Ruger pistol in case he and his brother were up to something and tucked it in my shorts, the handle pressing against the small of my back under the tank top. Then I headed downstairs.

I got out to the street and found the grinning Ebro in a B-Boy stance, one foot on the bumper of the Escalade.

"Goddamn boy, you done got swole on they ass!" Ebro laughed, clapping his hands together.

I cracked a smile and leaned on the Mustang. "Yeah, I had to grow up out here. You getting tatted up, I see."

"Yeah... I designed all of em myself," Ebro said, pulling his collar down and sleeve up to reveal several neck and arm tattoos. This you?" Ebro pointed at the Mustang.

I nodded. "Yeah, I'm done with the big bodies for a minute."

"I bet this boy gets up though, huh? I ain't even know you could drive a stick."

"Shoot, I didn't either," I said, chuckling. "I always wanted one, though, so I found it online, went to Florida to cop it, and taught myself how to drive it in a parking lot next to the dealer."

Ebro shook his head, smiling. "Smart ass Suede. Good to see you doing good, bruh."

I nodded and looked down. "Yup. Well, I gotta get to work in a minute, bruh. I'll catch you later."

We dapped like we did when we were kids, a handshake in between a brief bro hug.

I returned to my apartment, set my gun on the coffee table, and exhaled.

The Aftermath

Ebro Rabbani was my introduction to what genius looked like in action. Like most people, I once thought genius had to do with IQ and SAT scores. Instead, I learned from watching Ebro that genius is the ability to consistently and effectively put your talent to work. Everyone has million-dollar ideas. Many of us probably have ten of them a day. Genius lies in bringing those ideas to life.

Ebro was smart and maybe crazy enough to bring some wild ideas to life, and he changed many people's lives in the process — all before the age of 25.

The can't-miss Rabbani combo of business acumen, looks, and charm that we all thought would propel Hajj and Ebro to the highest heights found its way to his younger sisters, Halima and Khatiymah. They added what they learned from Brother Abdullah and Ebro and turned it into multi-million dollar hair, cosmetics, and jewelry empires.

Unfortunately, when Ebro lost the team that happily propped him up as the face of R. World, he lost his way. That boldness and hyperactive imagination unchecked landed him on the wrong side of the law throughout his late twenties and early thirties. Perhaps the trauma of losing Hajj and Sister Khansa was simply too much for him to overcome without professional help. Self-medication is rarely dosed correctly.

Ebro is a free man today, still charming his way into desirable rooms and trying to recapture that R. World magic from two decades ago. I'm rooting for him from afar. He'll always be my brother. And growing up, he was an absolute Giant in My Midst.

GIANT PRINCIPLE:

Be Bold like Ebro. Keep your childlike creativity as long as you can. Then, build the best team and keep your aces in their places.

Chapter 11:
Farouq Dawud

The best part about Abu marrying
Sister Mashallah was my favorite
play cousin becoming a real cousin.

For those unfamiliar with the Black American family structure, all of our parents' friends are aunties and uncles. So naturally, this makes their children our cousins, full stop. Similarly, in Islam, every elder is titled Ami or Amiti in some places, Brother or Sister in others, but effectively they are aunts and uncles. Taking it further than Black American culture, Muslim aunties and uncles' children are our Brothers and Sisters in Islam. So Black American Muslim kids growing up in the same community are already thisclose to being siblings with no blood or marital ties. Add in marriage, and all bets are off. We dismiss any qualifiers like step, second, removed, etc., and would pass a lie detector test asserting we are cousins or siblings with flying colors.

Sister Mashallah's sister Mumina had a son named Ahmad Farouq, who I had become close with back in the 6th grade when we first moved to Atlanta. Everyone called him Farouq (Fah-rūk). Although I had become Zak's shadow, I wasn't cool enough to be his true peer in those early days. While Zak was an ambassador and gracious host to me, a more natural friendship formed between Farouq and me based on commonality. Farouq was not shy but was a little awkward, so his attempts at being serious or humorous were often met with teasing. He had a nasal, high-pitched voice and was his elderly parents' only son, which meant his interests and tastes were slightly different than the rest of our peers.

The first time I visited Farouq's house, he was in the middle of a simulated chess game on his mother's computer. He had an older sister, Jamie, but she had moved out, so Farouq was, for all intents and purposes, an only child who taught himself how to play many games this way. I challenged him to a match, and we played for hours. He'd beat me using proven techniques made famous by grandmasters, and I'd beat him with unpredictability and creativity. I learned a plethora of new openings, defenses, and attacks straight out of the book playing against Farouq, and I'm sure he learned how to better exploit human weaknesses from me. As a result, we both became nearly unbeatable among the handful of chess players in the West End.

Farouq would visit my house and jump right in with our role-playing games. He was versatile, taking on a country western accent to play a fictitious country music star named Sig Sour being interviewed about his new album or a New York accent to impersonate Eddie Torres from New York undercover. He kept the Sig nickname long after the tape recorders stopped rolling. He fit well with my siblings and was the first person I imagined being ok with Najwa marrying. So we were united in our awkward, intelligent, not locked into inner city Black boy trope ways.

Farouq's parents separated around the same time Umi and Abu did, leaving him as the man of the house and caretaker for his elderly and often sick mother. It forced him to grow up with seriousness and develop a hustle mentality. He kept a job, paid bills, and tolerated no jokes about his mother. There were occasions when he'd fight because of a perceived slight of her. Farouq and sister Muminah moved away to the eastside in our mid-teens, around the same time I was kicking it with Khalfani heavy. When he started coming back around a few years later, he was as changed as I was.

Although I visited Farouq and Sister Muminah a few times after Eids during those eastside years, I didn't see him enough to witness his growth firsthand. When Farouq made his official return to the West End at 17, it was almost a Steve Urkel to Stephon Urkelle type of glow-up. He had grown to about 6'1, with no awkwardness, was smooth with the ladies, and was a phenomenal basketball player. He had honed his charm at a sales job and used it to talk his way into a rental car hookup from a manager. Rolling through the West End in a brand new drop-top Chrysler Sebring in the summer of 1999, it was clear the old Farouq was gone forever. Sorta.

Farouq being the selfless people pleaser that he was, it didn't take long before all of his friends were pushing the latest Chrysler 300Ms, Concords, and Sebrings through the city, myself included. The hookup had a little grey area to it, as most hookups usually do, and we were supposed to return the cars within 30-60 days. But no one did. Instead, people found drive-out dealer tags and chop shops that allowed them to drive the car longer, sell it, or both. Farouq handled the heat from the fired rental car manager privately and never brought it to anyone's attention.

Farouq loved seeing his friends happy, so he took one for the team.

Farouq and I would race our drop-tops down I-20 East from Ashby street to Panola road to visit a pair of sisters we liked, hitting 120 MPH on straightaways and 70 MPH with no brakes on curves with 25 MPH speed limits. Could we have ridden together? Of course. But where's the fun in that? We preferred pulling up back to back with the tops down, with me blasting something unconventional like Will You Be There by Michael Jackson, while Farouq's go-to was This Woman's Work by Maxwell. The further from No Limit and Three Six Mafia, the better. The rule at stoplights was you either had to sing the song at the top of your lungs or just look hard and mean mug any pedestrians while the R&B or alternative rock music blasted. Either way, you could not crack a smile.

Left to right Top: Ebro, Jamil, Me, Farouq, Shaakir, Harun
Left to right Bottom: Bishara and Ahmad

Farouq and Sister Muminah settled into a duplex on Oak Street around the corner from Abu Shaka's house. I could see their front door from my room's window. The duplex was about five houses west of The Shed, and the inhabitant of the other side of the duplex, a kid our age from New York named Dennis, was a hooper as well. So Farouq spent a lot of time at the Shed working on and showing off his game. Whether in one-on-ones with Dennis, 21 with us both, or five-on-fives with the adults, I got the sense that Farouq's growth on the basketball court was symbolic of his growth in every other facet of his life. And he loved being the high jumping, versatile alpha he had become on the court.

The Call

One afternoon, I was at work at the Hampton, carrying extra towels up the stairs to a guest room. I always took the stairs because it kept me in shape, and there were no cameras in the stairwell. I may have been shedding some of my introverted ways, but I still avoid being watched if I can help it. On my way down to the lobby, I felt something I couldn't explain. I sat down at the bottom of the stairwell and buried my head in my lap, probably for 5-10 minutes, breathing deeply, trying to collect myself. I wasn't tired, nauseous, or sick, but I couldn't move. Finally, I got up and returned to the front desk, where my two concerned-looking co-workers, Mignon and Angel, greeted me.

"Where have you been?!" Mignon asked.

"The phone has been ringing off the hook for you," Angel said.

"I was just… I don't… who was it? Who called?" I mustered.

Angel replied, "Some guy named Cal… cal um… funny? He called like six times."

"Here he is right here," Mignon said, frantically handing me the front desk phone.

"Saalaykum?" I said reluctantly.

"Walaikum salaam. Farouq got shot."

I recognized Khalfani's voice but needed to process the words he was saying.

"Huh? What? Where?"

"He was at the shed, and some dude sprayed the court up after a fight," Khalfani explained calmly. "Farouq got hit pushing little Nardin and Ibn out the way."

"Where is he now?" I asked, ignoring the line of guests forming in front of me.

"They took him to Grady. He was talking when they put him in the ambulance, but we're all headed there now."

"Alright, saalaykum."

I hung up the phone, apologized to an understanding Mignon and Angel, grabbed my keys and phone from the back office, and sprinted to my car. My mind flooded with memories of the night Hajj died, and my eyes filled with tears while my foot mashed the gas pedal, ignoring that my license was suspended for failure to appear in court for a speeding ticket. Once out of the downtown streets and onto the freeway, I banged on the steering wheel, intermittently reciting Qur'an and screaming curse words.

Grady

Grady Hospital has the best trauma response unit in the state of Georgia. Similar to how criminals joked about preferring Atlanta's Pretrial Detention Center to Fulton County's Rice Street, they would often joke about making sure they go to Grady if they get shot. Even if you must pass Emory, Atlanta Medical Center, and South Fulton Hospitals on the way, Grady was where you wanted to be after getting shot. Grady also had the distinction of being proof of being a true ATLien, if you were a Grady Baby. So Farouq being at Grady lent a sense of comfort to the frightening scenario. When I walked into the waiting room, I saw Zak, Khalfani, Ebro, Yaseen, and most of Atlanta's Muslim community in shock and disarray.

As with Hajj, Farouq was universally loved and considered one of the community's brightest young stars. No way Allah would end both of their lives as teenagers, right? I thought.

All this thinking, processing, hoping, and praying was unlike when Hajj died. Hajj was already gone when we arrived on the scene. The longer we prayed for Farouq and waited for an answer, the longer we knew he was alive.

Finally, the surgeon came down and said the surgery was successful. The bullet had entered his abdomen and ricocheted up through his torso and out of his shoulder/neck area. But he assured us that Farouq was fighting and in good shape, all things considered. He upgraded Farouq from critical to serious condition, and everyone breathed a sigh of relief. We hugged each other, some smiling, others crying, everyone holding on a little tighter for a little longer than usual.

Ebro, Fakeer, Shakir, and I decided to get something to eat before returning to spend the night in the waiting room. We ate, then I decided to go home and change out of my work uniform. When I got home, I had to tell a terrified Umi that it sounded like Farouq was going to be ok, but I was going back to the hospital. I had to try and hold it together while she squeezed me and told me she loved me. I was seven inches taller than her by this time, but she may as well have been rocking me in her arms.

"I know, Umi. I love you too," was all I could muster in a shaky voice.

I changed, made salat and an extra long du'a for Farouq, then went into the kitchen to grab some snacks for the night before heading back to Grady.

Then my cell phone rang. I recognized the number as Shakir's house phone.

"Saalaykum…" I said quizzically, wondering why Shakir wasn't calling me from his cell.

It turns out it was Siddiq, Shakir's younger brother.

146

"Wallaykum salaam… Ay Suede. He didn't make it. Farouq gone, man."

I just hung up.

I crumbled against the laundry room wall and let out the loudest scream.

Umi knew instantly what it meant and immediately came into the room and smothered me with an embrace.

I soaked her shirt with my tears for five minutes before anger started to mix in with my sadness.

"Why does this keep happening??" I cried.

"Why can't Allah take the bad ones??"

"He didn't even do anything. Farouq never bothered ANYONE, MAN!!!

"What's the point of even trying to do anything? I'm just gonna get killed anyway!!"

"The ones like me all die!!!"

Poor Umi couldn't stand to hear her youngest son say these things and encouraged me to lie down, as she did when I got angry as a child. Instead, I stood up and bolted out of the house, where Bobbi waited outside in her Blue Ford Explorer. We drove around the corner to the shed, where we reminisced on Farouq as a third wheel, examined the crime scene, and cried together. It was one of the last times I cried in my life.

Nothing has been able to move, shock,
or scare me nearly as much as
Hajj and Farouq dying as teens did.

The Two Outcomes

In Islam, it is Sunnah (a practice of the Prophet Muhammad) to bury the dead within three days of their passing. We don't do embalming fluids or fancy caskets so that the body can decompose back into the earth as naturally as possible, among other reasons. While this makes it easier for the family to afford the Janazah (funeral) and expedites any closure that the rituals mentioned above may bring, it can be stressful to coordinate the travel arrangements, repass, prayer service, and burial within 24-48 hours. Especially when a large portion of the family is not Muslim and complains at every turn.

Farouq's family was prepared for the news of death but assumed it would be that of Sister Muminah due to her advanced age and battles with various ailments. Farouq confided in me about the possibility often. But no one is ever prepared when a senseless act of violence rips away their bright young star of a son. So I pledged to Sister Muminah that I would do anything she needed me to take some of her burdens off.

She held my face and beamed, "Oh Masood, Farouq loved you so much. And I know you loved him. Don't worry about him. He died as a martyr saving those two young men." Her smile while she said this conveyed her conviction that it was true.

"You are an excellent writer. Write about your Brother. We need an obituary created for him, and I know you will create a beautiful one. I may help you relieve some of this tension too."

She kissed me on the forehead, rubbed my shoulders, and I marched home with my orders.

Creating media in the days before Canva and graphic design apps meant going to Kinko's and literally copying and pasting pictures and words together. I wrote the obituary, found a good photo of Farouq, and planned on hitting the Kinko's downtown after Ebro and I hung out with Khetanya and her friend Karina. We ate at City Cafe Diner and hung out at Centennial Park before I announced that I needed to go to the 24-7 Kinko's at the Equitable building downtown. Khetanya rode with Ebro in his Blue 300M while Shakir and Karina hopped into my White Concourse with me.

Ebro was the one who introduced me to Kinko's back when the shop didn't have all the tools he needed to design. And later, when we came to alter our IDs so we could fly to New York alone before we turned 16. And finally, when my transcript needed a little editing when I was transferring from open campus to Washington High. So Ebro led the way through downtown Atlanta to the Equitable building with the speed of someone who had made that trek a thousand times because he had. I tailed him through an empty Five Points and made an ill-fated decision to run a light to keep up with him.

Bad Move.

A Georgia State University patrol car swooped in behind me from the cut and lit me up with blue and white lights. My heart jumped into my throat because my license was suspended after being caught in Peach County, Georgia doing 125 in a Dodge Caravan on the way home from Daytona earlier that year. The officer approached, and I confessed right away that I shouldn't have been driving but explained that I was going to make Farouq's obituary around the corner. I showed him the copy and the picture of Farouq, and Karina said she could drive the rest of the way.

It didn't work.

I went to jail for the first time in my life.

I spent the entire night awake in a holding cell, trying to convince every correctional officer there that I should be released to attend my cousin's funeral in the morning. I didn't have any more tears, though, so I was not convincing enough.

Finally, in the morning, the new shift supervisor heard my story, snapped at the entire staff for holding me, and let me go on my own recognizance at 9:15 AM, roughly around the same time Farouq was being lowered into his grave. I walked home from the pretrial detention center, kicking the same rock from Garnett Station to Holderness street.

I couldn't believe Farouq and I were the ones who became the literal embodiment of "Dead or In Jail."

Farouq was the one. The golden child. The star. I was very similar to him. If we fell victim to the two outcomes, the average kid in the hood didn't stand a chance. So I promised myself to try and make it to 25. Something told me that if I got to 25, Allah would give me at least until 40. I would get married, start a family and build things to help the next Farouq survive so the world could benefit from their light.

He was a Giant in My Midst.

GIANT PRINCIPLE:

Glow up NOW. You never know how much time you have to impact this earth.

PART II:
The Reform

At age 13, I was an innocent, quiet, straight-A student who had memorized a fifth of the Qur'an. By 16, I was a borderline dropout who was quick to fight, hang out with drug dealers and entertain the young women those sorts of things attracted. I still knew a fifth of the Qur'an; I just didn't have a relationship with it and was largely unimpressed by those around me who did. By 24, I was putting the pieces of my life back together and repairing my reputation.

Growth is seldom linear, and it would be inaccurate to say the Foundational Giants had no part in helping me change for the better. But the people in this section met me at my worst and chose to see and cultivate the good in me.

> Life comes at you fast in the hood.
> But with a broken family,
> it comes at you at deadly speed.

I was suspended nine times in the 9th grade, primarily for fighting and skipping school. I finished that year with a 0.667 GPA. My high school didn't want me back for my second year but reluctantly gave me one more chance when I returned from Detroit. But after being cornered by a group of guys I'd fought with the previous year and setting off a massive brawl, I was expelled from North Atlanta and sent to St. Luke's Academy.

St. Luke's Academy

St. Luke's was one of Atlanta's Communities in Schools drop-out prevention programs, where they focused on individual students and brought in community leaders to motivate us. One of those leaders was a man named Mr. Tony.

Mr. Tony would come in weekly with his pressed suit, cufflinks, and clean-shaven head and speak to us like men and women. He would give us a glimpse of what we could become if we took ourselves more seriously and managed time more effectively. I doubt Mr. Tony remembers me because he likely encountered hundreds of young men like me weekly. But I promised to pay it forward if I lived long enough, and nowadays, I jump at opportunities to be a Mr. Tony for the next generation of leaders.

St. Luke's smaller class sizes and individualized approach worked for me. As a result, I never got anything less than an A for the rest of my high school career. And on August 24, 1998, my principal, Ms. Emma Mack, selected me to be featured on Fox 5 Atlanta's Good Morning Atlanta as an example of the effectiveness of the alternative school system. I still had no idea what I wanted to become, but as I sat in the make-up artists' chair, listening to the hosts tell the audience about me, I decided to live up to my potential.

Systemic Survival

Once I decided to live up to my potential, I had to develop a system. I mapped out a strict diet, workout regimen, and budget from which I would not deviate. I designed the system to keep me out of fight-or-flight and kill-or-be-killed situations while putting myself in positions to work on my deficiencies and meet people from other walks of life. So anything that could lead to an encounter with a cop was out. I knew a lot of guys that would scream F the police at the top of their lungs but then stand on the corner slanging crack all day, and I could not understand it. That's like saying you hate linebackers, then choosing to be a running back. I hated linebackers, so I decided to play a different sport altogether.

The relationship between criminals and cops is a sport where the players try to beat the Bizarro World versions of themselves.

They both have the same adrenaline addiction and think they are above the law. They both study the rules and history of the game incessantly and learn to think like the other side. When you think about it, they are more like colleagues than adversaries. But I could not stand being in the presence of cops after a few encounters with Atlanta's Red Dog unit and had a hard time not poking at their insecurities while being questioned by them. So I preferred to stay far away from things that meant meeting more cops.

I liked to hang out with Ebro and the R. World boys and Shobe and the Atwood boys, but not nearly as much as they liked to hang out with each other. It always made me a little more of an outsider than everyone else in the group. But when I decided I wanted to survive the hood with no diseases, injuries, or criminal record, I knew I needed to put even more space between myself and the cliques.

Idle time with big groups of young men in the hood was often interrupted by fights, gunshots, cops, or all three. The later in the night it got, the worse it was.

That's why I kept a job working the 3 pm - 11 pm front desk shift at a Hampton Inn. That shift kept me out of the streets during prime killing hours and still allowed me to have a life outside of work if I was disciplined enough to go to sleep when I got home. I kept hearing I had the skill set to become a journalist, attorney, or businessman, but I had to not die to become any of those things. Besides, I still needed to improve critical things, such as making eye contact, projecting my voice, and being consistent. So I got to work on those things each time I checked someone in — close to 200 times per week. I had to answer the phone with a smile probably 1,000 more times per week. After a while, I had an entirely extroverted persona that I could use when needed. It almost felt like cheating that I was getting paid to better myself.

Black Women Saved My Life

Every time one of my friends got shot,
stabbed, or arrested, I would have
been there if not for work or women.

To explore all sides of myself as an adult after moving out on my own, I needed to tap back into the innocence and freedom I enjoyed running across that field when I was six. Instead, the life I had sunk into was suffocating me like the well. I needed to be around people who would watch Jeopardy and Seinfeld or sing Goo Goo Dolls songs at the top of their lungs with me. I had interests and tastes such as art, film, writing, history, and alternative and rock music that mostly lay dormant while I was with the homies.

I had become so good at acting like a piranha
that my inner goldfish was nearly gone.

I could get to know and be myself around women more naturally than I could with the homies. It made sense – I was a mama's boy, Najwa was my best friend, and counting Abu Shaka's daughters Taharah and Shakeelah, I had six sisters total. And consistently, the only friends who checked on me at my lowest points through the years were the female ones.

Once in place, my system left little time for anything outside my hustle and the hotel. Sometimes I flipped cars that I'd buy from the auction. Other times, I hit the road to vend at Mardi Gras in New Orleans or St. Patrick's Day in Savannah. I liked being the hotel hookup guy for my friends because it validated my increasingly more prolonged absences, but even on my off days, I was spending more time with the friends who called up to my job and asked me what I wanted to eat. Or the ones who, when I was in between cars, asked if I needed a ride. The ones who bought tickets to an indie film festival so I could see what kinds of scripts were winning best original screenplay.

They just so happened to all be women.

Islam advocates supervision for all non-marital male/female interaction, and by no means is this section encouragement for younger Muslims who may read this to have girlfriends or boyfriends. But I moved out of the house at 17, and as an ambitious, single man in Atlanta, women keeping me out of serious trouble was my reality.

To Parents of Muslim teenagers: I strongly recommend that you find ways to allow them to interact with the opposite sex in more meaningful ways than awkward "sit-downs" where four adults pepper two kids with questions about marriage.

Seeking Half My Deen

There is a principle in Islam that says, "marriage is half your deen." Deen is often interpreted as religion, but the more accurate definition is 'way of life.' Islam leaves no stone on the road to success unturned from the cradle to the grave, but marriage unlocks half of them. No sooner than Muslim kids turn 13, grow a little peach fuzz, or buy a training bra, they start hearing this golden adage from every adult with their best interest at heart. Even when you become educated, gain degrees, and earn large salaries, the elders scoff at your attempts to develop a voice within the community if you are unmarried. Meanwhile, the community lauds marriages between two teenagers or even a teenager and an adult.

I get it. Communities are a collection of families, and good families start with good men and women. So a leader who goes home to people of various ages from both sexes will consider more sides of an issue than someone who lives alone with their thoughts. But there is more to a sustainable marriage than good intentions. Unfortunately, I learned this the hard way.

Shady Roots

After spending ages 16-20 swearing up and down that I was going to marry Bobbi, when it came down to discussing what such a union would look like, we discovered that we were equally unyielding. I was not willing to compromise any of my Islamic faith, nor was she her Baptist Christian faith. Bobbi and I had spent the better part of five years ignoring the aspects of our religions that would have prevented us from carrying on in the manner we did. Still, we were unwilling to imagine our children experiencing a different upbringing than our own. She wanted to sing hymns from the pew on Sundays and unwrap boxes under the tree on Christmas mornings. In contrast, I wanted a household where Jesus was nothing more or less than a respected Prophet, and the Qur'an was the final authority. And speaking of Qur'an, since Abu made me memorize a chunk of it, I was going to pass that on too.

Yet, despite its shady roots, our relationship didn't feel like it was evil or grounds for punishment.

I'd rationalize with myself:

Bobbi was my best friend, muse, and sister. All rolled up in one person.

We developed our personalities together.

If not for her, I probably would have had dozens of inappropriate relationships between ages 16 and 20, not just one.

There is no telling what I might have done if left to my devices during difficult times, like when Hajj and Farouq died, had Bobbi not been around.

She made me a better person and protected me from rash decisions that could have gotten me killed.

In return, I helped her through some of her dark times.

That has to be Qadr, right?

When we became mature enough in our respective faiths to stop justifying our relationship, Bobbi and I begrudgingly went our separate ways. With the dead-serious caveat that we would tie the knot, no matter what, if we were both unmarried by the time she turned 27. In Islam, men can marry the People of the Book (devout Christians and Jews), and Bobbi had proven to be a person of her book when she chose it over me.

Player Rumors

When Bobbi season was over, I naively expected the ones to follow to be the same. After being introduced to relationships the way I was, I found it difficult to be casual or hot/cold with new women I was interested in. As a result, I was more forward, expressive, vulnerable, and interested in what they liked than their other suitors. These factors, combined with my independence, led to multiple women seeing me as husband material and, thus, a target.

Some older people within the Atlanta Muslim community held my adolescence against me. They cited my notorious fighting phase, my dope boy Atwood days, R. World's promotion of hood culture, and the use of scantily clad women in advertisements as proof of my loose morals. But those things, coupled with my presence at the Masjid and Islamic knowledge, only bolstered my resume with their daughters. They didn't want a holier-than-thou square who their father was more in love with than they were. Plus, unlike their parents, they knew I was the 'different' one in all of those situations.

Whatever Muslim girls liked, the non-Muslim girls loved. So shortly after moving out of Umi and Abu Shaka's house, I found myself fighting "player" rumors and under pressure to choose the lifestyle and reputation I wanted to carry throughout my adulthood.

Bermudian Balance

The closest thing that Ebro had to therapy after Sister Khansa passed was Shanon, a sweet Bermudian girl he met at a conference in Chicago and married a few weeks later. Shanon had recently converted to Islam but was devout in her approach to learning and applying it to her life. She gave Ebro advice for the R. World's women's lines, and her modesty even rubbed off on him a little. Shanon balanced Ebro out and filled some of the maternal void left by Sister Khansa, not just for Ebro but for the whole clique. Fakeer, Hudhayfah, and I all lived within a block of Ebro. Soon after Shanon moved in, we'd gather for dinner at their fragrant, comfortable, well-decorated apartment several times a week, then return to our stale, bare-walled bachelor pads. Ebro was noticeably more healthy, focused and mature, and his marriage to Shanon was a ringing endorsement of the "half your deen" axiom for us all.

I was young, handsome, and hood rich, and I didn't want to lose my religion. But I was overwhelmed by temptation at 4Zero4 Sports, the rap videos, photo shoots, and anywhere I could be observed jumping out of my Cadillac on chrome fresh as hell. True to form, Ahmad already knew who he would marry and when – Nena Madyun from Atlanta Masjid, after he finished college. Fakeer, Hudhayfah, and I were all more open to persuasion. But to a man, we were inspired by Ebro and Shanon's marriage and decided we needed to find Shanons and Nenas of our own. It didn't take long to realize my options for marriage were not quite as extensive as those for casual dating.

The most logical were either too close, almost like sisters. Or my friends' actual sisters, or my sisters' friends. Or too far – Suki had moved back to New York at the time. And Shanon was a girl from a small island who Ebro met out of town, so it seemed like the best route was to find a pretty, modest stranger who didn't already have preconceived notions about you from childhood.

Z Girl

In those days, a Sister named Amber Khan threw the biggest and best Eid parties for young Muslims in Atlanta. They were always creative and fun and allowed young adult Muslims to be themselves in a halal (kosher/permissible) mixed gathering. Amber rented out a club downtown that year, and the party had a DJ, various icebreaker games, and a Madden tournament. The winner of the Madden tournament got a new Playstation 2, so I signed up and won. When Amber announced the winner and presented me with the prize, I said a few words to the crowd of young Muslims and got a good look at how everyone was looking at me. So I wasn't surprised at the end of the event when Amber pulled me aside and said a particular Sister named Zakiya was interested in me. I had never seen her before and could tell she was very modest by the style of her khimar (scarf/hijab). But I liked how she kept looking at me even when she lowered her gaze, and I thought she looked the part of a young Muslim wife. So I told Amber I was down to have a conversation with Zakiya and to hook it up.

In the following weeks, I went on a few heavily chaperoned dates with Zakiya, her sister, her friend, and Hudhayfah. After all, as we were taught, if an unmarried man and woman are alone together, the third party is Shaitaan. Although it was pretty clear Zakiya and I didn't have anything in common except being young Muslims who desired to be married, the distractions and sidebar conversations with all the other people around us masked it. Hudhayfah married Zakiya's friend after a few weeks, and Shanon took her under her wing, adding to the internal pressure I felt to complete the trifecta.

Zakiya's father came down to meet me during NBA All-Star weekend and found me selling $1500 leather Jeff Hamilton coats to the show-offs near Centennial park like they were cold water on a hot day. I threw in a little adab (good manners), flattery, and tajweed (proper Arabic pronunciation) and got his blessing to marry Zakiya.

Finally, on a random Tuesday night in March, I dressed up in a white thobe with a white kufi and a red kifaya - my best Muslim costume - and married a girl I didn't know. All because she checked off a few boxes.

I took my new bride to the grocery store on the second night of our marriage. I filled the cart with all my favorite Bachelor foods and told her to grab anything else she needed to make my kitchen ours. We went down every store aisle and picked up spices, powders, grains, and vegetables I had never considered buying myself. We even got some kitchenware and appliances. The girl knew her way around a kitchen, and we filled the cart beyond its capacity. I sensed her excitement with each addition and realized it was an introduction to adulthood and the level of freedom I had enjoyed for four years. It felt nice being able to do that for her.

Then, pulling into the checkout line, I invited her to play a game.

"Guess how much all this is going to cost? Whoever's guess is closest wins," I said.

Zakia scanned the basket with her eyes, looked at me, giggled, shrugged, and guessed, "Ninety dollars?"

I laughed until I saw she was dead serious and felt my heart sink.

After paying $345 for the contents of that basket, I checked out.

Checked out of thinking her innocence was charming or pretending we matched, that is. Zakiya was 18, and I knew that was young, but I was only 21 and had not signed up to raise a child.

During the silent drive home, I realized we would not be married long.

I felt sorry for Zakiya as soon as I arrived at this conclusion, but I had to be honest with myself. My attempts to converse with Zakiya about my workdays never went anywhere, and I spent far too much time playing Madden or hanging out at Faqeer's house in the weeks following the wedding to avoid our awkward conversations. She was raised to be an obedient, domestic Muslim housewife, and she killed it in those roles. Our apartment was always spotless, dinner was always hot and ready when I came home from work, and she didn't have a combative bone in her body. Plus, that star-struck, doe-eyed look she had at the Eid party never left her face when she looked at me. I was an absolute superstar to her, and whenever I walked in the door, sat down to eat, dressed, or anything, she would stare at me as if she couldn't believe she got me.

But at 21, none of those things mattered to me. I would rather pay a housekeeper and go out to eat with a woman who stimulated my mind and challenged me. Zakiya and I were not equally yoked. I couldn't believe she got me either.

Two months into the marriage, I called Umi and expressed my frustrations about being married to Zakiya.

"I know, son. She's a sweet girl, but she's not your type." Umi said matter of factly.

"You just have to be honest with her and end it before you get her pregnant."

So I did.

To divorce in Islam, you must go through a celibate three-month grace period called Iddat. Including that period, Zakiya and I were married for five months. But the state of Georgia was never involved, so it was a clean break aside from the awkward drive back to her home state up north. Zakiya's father didn't seem upset, though. On the contrary, when I entered the family home, he and some of Zakiya's sisters seemed grateful that I gave her a chance, which made me wonder if I was missing a critical piece of information about her.

But still, the failure was mine. I had arrogantly assumed I could make any relationship work with sheer will. I regret that I embarrassed Zakiya and probably scarred her for life by not giving my full attention to vetting a life partner and then running at the first sign of difficulty. Those five months were not my proudest moment. The silver lining was I learned the seriousness of marriage.

And I vowed not to repeat any of those same mistakes.

In This Section

The giants in this section are the ones who helped me become intentional about tapping into my potential as a leader. In addition, these people helped me course-correct the components that suffered most during my troubled adolescence: education and faith.

Chapter 12:
Ariaka Autry

The early twenties are a time for
exploration and discovery.

Some people shed their high school personas and try on brand-new ones in college. Others find odd jobs to fund a passion or a soul-searching summer trip to Spain or Thailand. But for some of us, the early twenties was simply a time to begin our careers. When I moved into my 4th Ward apartment shortly before my 18th birthday, it didn't take long to come to grips with the reality that if I didn't remember to pay my electric bill, my lights would get cut off. That freedom is an illusion if it means neglecting responsibility.

That, if I don't hustle, I don't eat.

Despite scoring 1460 on the SAT and being recruited by and accepted to several Ivy League schools, college wasn't a serious consideration for me. Instead, I dove into the business world with Ebro and company. Around the time R. World was generating buzz as we began to lock in more and more wholesale accounts in Atlanta and the surrounding area, I saw an opportunity to retail our products. So we opened up 4Zero4 Sports, a clothing store, as a side hustle. Located inside an indoor flea market in downtown Atlanta, 4Zero4 Sports was a convenient way for me to earn more money while learning about the retail side of the business. But it quickly became a course on networking as I formed relationships with the other shop owners.

Located in the most visible space in the entire market, 4Zero4 was the first thing anyone would see when they entered. There were only a few places in the whole mall that you could get to without passing us first. So I would get a good long look at the hustlers, rappers, movers, and shakers in the up-and-coming hip-hop Mecca as they came in and out of the notorious shopping destination. But most importantly to me at the time, they got a good look at *me* in my element, modeling my exclusive merchandise and getting money.

Of all the people I met during that time, the one that stood out the most was the owner of a small women's clothing boutique downstairs from my store called Glam Rocks. Her name was Ariaka (pronounced Erica) Autry.

The first time I saw Ariaka, mine was probably the twentieth pair of eyes on her as she strode swiftly past the shops toward mine. Oversized shades still on, a big designer purse across her shoulder, and big hair bouncing, she loudly greeted her admirers with a grand smile. But she never slowed down to entertain any responses. Seeing how accustomed she was to getting attention, I turned my back to speak to my employee when she got close. I don't think he heard anything I was saying as he watched her go down the steps to her store.

She was *that* chick.

When I sensed the coast was clear, I saw the property manager, the mixtape store owner, the young Senegalese merchant, and a market regular heading my way. They had each made it their business to give me the lay of the land since my opening day, and educating me on what I had just witnessed was a point of emphasis for them all.

During the impromptu briefing, I learned that Ariaka had these guys eating out of the palm of her hand using only smoke and mirrors. Let them tell it, she was either a mob boss's girlfriend or cousin, but she dated a famous rapper who would show up at her store now and then. Oh, and her store was a front operation for both of them, but she was also an exotic dancer.

In other words, they had no clue who she was or how she lived her life, but they had all tried hard to find out, to no avail.

The one thing they were sure of was that there was no point in me ever going down there to talk to her because she didn't give dudes like us the time of day.

"Us?" I thought...

In the following weeks, I gathered why Ariaka was the queen of that mall. First, that smile was ever-present whether she spoke with a man, woman, customer, employee, or whoever. Anyone in her presence felt special because she would turn on the smile and engage them in an animated but sincere tone. The second reason was that she spoke in vague terms and pivoted like a seasoned politician when anyone pried into her personal life. So even when she was rejecting a suitor, it looked and sounded more like a cat and mouse game. However, the third reason was most striking:

The young lady was simply great at business.

The first time I decided to check out Glam Rocks was when R. World had a photoshoot coming up, and we needed something for the female models to wear. At this point, R. World was buzzing a little in the streets, but it was primarily due to the sales of our signature men's A-Town shirts. After our first Magic Show, we knew that if we were ever going to be as big as Sean John or South Pole, we would have to sell to women too.

R. World was departing from our innocent beginnings with the new women's line marketing campaign. So this photo shoot would include me, Ebro, and several female models. These photos needed to be a little more risque than our only women's shirt design allowed.

I had noticed Glam Rocks customers leaving with customized women's dresses made from men's t-shirts. So I decided to ask Ariaka to customize a few of our A-Town shirts similarly. After inspecting myself in the 4Zero4 Sports try-on mirror, I walked down to Glam Rocks with my business face on.

I didn't always turn my back on Ariaka when she walked by each morning, but I did not give her as much attention as she was used to over the first few weeks of being open. So when I walked into the store, Ariaka looked up from her book and raised her eyebrows.

"Hello, welcome to Glam Rocks!" she chirped, ignoring her employee, who was eyeballing her with a smirk.

I said, "Hey, thanks… you guys convert shirts into custom dresses for women, right?"

She looked around at the custom dresses lining the walls of her store as if to say, "well, duh," but responded, "We sure do!" with that big smile.

Smiling and shaking my head, I said, "Okay, good, my name is Masood, and I'm with R. World Shirt Company. We also have the store upstairs from you."

Her employee offered her hand and said, "Hey, Masood!" with a big grin. Ariaka introduced her employee as Melissa and said she was the one I needed to talk to.

I shook Melissa's hand and explained what the dresses were for. I told them I wanted at least one of the dresses to look like the UNC jersey dress worn by R&B singer Mya in the video for her song Best of Me, which featured Jay-Z. Then, turning to Ariaka, I asked, "Have you ever seen that video?"

Ariaka looked a lot like Mya, and I was sure she had heard it a lot.

She tilted her head to the side a little and gave me a dead-eyed look that said, 'really?' But responded, "yes, we can do that for you, no problem."

She wrote an invoice and told me they would be ready in a week. "Just bring the shirts you want to use, and we can get started right away!"

Glam Rocks turned half a dozen of our A-Town shirts into six sleek, A-Town dresses that made our photoshoot and subsequent marketing campaign a hit. One of our employees at the time — a nice girl named Summer Walker, filled in for one of the models that day, and the photos of her in the dresses helped her launch a very successful video modeling career.

Everything went smoothly, and I saw that I could learn a lot from Ariaka about organization and planning.

A few days after the business was complete, Ariaka and I had lunch at a new deli that had opened up not far from the mall. I learned that Ariaka had no intention of going to college either. But unlike me, she was not in the least bit insecure about it.

Instead, she read books on business, ethics, sociology, finance, and God. She planned every detail of her life months, even years in advance. She even practiced those slip tactics I'd observed in the hallway.

My system was elementary compared to hers.

We started exchanging books and our thoughts on them, beginning with Robert Greene's The 48 Laws of Power. She was adamant that principle number 1 of the 48 Laws, Never Outshine the Master, was designed to test your mastery of laws 2-48. "If you get the rest down, YOU the master! Shine!" She would scream. Later, I stole her book on Ethics as an elaborate joke.

This period is what re-awakened the reader in me. It was a key reminder that I opted out of college, not education. As I attempted to jump from hustler to entrepreneur and finally business owner, I needed to read, plan, practice, and pray like Ariaka to pull it off.

Over the years, Ariaka has built several successful real estate and finance businesses. But she found her niche in the import hair business with her company Virgin Hair Depot. On Dec. 25, 2017, Ariaka inked a deal that made her the first African American woman to own a factory in Henan, China. This deal enabled her to scale Virgin Hair Depot via franchises, memberships, subscriptions, courses, and her personal brand. In short, **Ariaka** built an empire by mastering her Glam Rocks hustle. Find her on social media as Ariaka Daily, to see a self-made woman shine.

GIANT PRINCIPLE:

Seek relevant Knowledge and apply it daily, like Ariaka. Don't let your enrollment status interfere with your education.

GIANT PRINCIPLE:

Plan your work and work your plan.

Once I began reading, planning, and practicing like Ariaka, I started planning my life around the five prescribed prayers. At first, they may as well have been yoga or tantric breathing exercises. Beneficial, but superficial. With my renewed intention, they became easier to perform on time, but I needed more sincerity and devotion. I was still the Muslim Abu made me, not the Muslim I needed to be.

My relationships with the following four rightly guided Imams helped me develop a sincere dialogue with and understanding of Allah.

Chapter 13:
Imam Siraj Wahhaj

Siraj Wahhaj
Imam, Masjid Taqwa

Imam Siraj Wahhaj may be the only man standing at the crossroad between Imam Jamil Al-Amin, Imam Warith Deen Mohammed, and Minister Louis Farrakhan.

He does so while being equally revered by not only those men's communities but the entire Muslim world.

From Jeffery 12X to Siraj Wahhaj, Arabic for Bright Light, this man learned how to live, speak, and lead from and with those three titans. But he brought his own Brooklyn flavor to the recipe.

Crack cocaine was a nuclear bomb designed to decimate the black community in the 1980s. New York City was ground zero. The cheap, easy-to-make concoction created two types of fiends - the user and the seller: the high chaser and the clout chaser. Once sufficiently hooked, the government swept in and sent both types to prison. Imam Siraj's fellow Brooklynite Jay-Z said, "They gave us drugs, then turned around and investigated us."

It was war.

Not on drugs but on the Black community itself. The Black family crumbled because of the staggering amount of would-be fathers, protectors, and providers taken away. Chaos, bloodshed, and anarchy are what ensued.

But Imam Siraj was not one to stand idly by.

He created a Sutra team, or task force, to rid his community of drug dealers and users since the police didn't show interest in doing it themselves. They did so with such effectiveness that a group of drug dealers once called the police on Imam Siraj and his team.

The effort to clear the block of drugs was successful, and Imam Siraj's Masjid Taqwa became the center of a vibrant community rife with industry and family life. This model of taking charge of securing the community when the police showed they were not interested was successfully replicated up and down both coasts.

One such place was Atlanta, in Imam Jamil's community, where I learned of Imam Siraj. Imam Jamil casts a long shadow, literally and figuratively. He did not often share the podium with guest speakers but happily stood aside whenever Imam Siraj came to town.

When Imam Siraj Speaks, those who have heard him before kinda tip you off that you're in for a treat by smiling, fixing their attention on his face, and leaning in. The first time I experienced this, I looked around and then back at Imam Siraj, waiting to be dazzled.

He didn't disappoint then and hasn't to this day.

His speaking style is charismatic storytelling in a low tone, followed by booming punchlines and scriptures. When he gets rolling, anyone succumbing to sermon sleepiness is startled awake, wondering what the commotion is. Once he gets everyone's attention, he'll inject humor and tie everything together with a soft voice.

I was a quiet kid that was good with words but terrible at public speaking, so I wanted to study Imam Siraj's speaking style. For years, anytime I came across a cd of one of his lectures, I would buy it and listen to it over and over. I began to memorize some parts.

In 2017, the community that I helped lead celebrated building a new masjid from the ground up with a Grand Opening fundraiser event. I helped secure Imam Siraj as the keynote speaker.

Growing up in Atlanta and working on the hip-hop industry's periphery, I always met stars and was never fazed. You name the star with Atlanta ties, I either knew or worked with them. Of course, I respected their hustle, but up close, they looked and felt just like another one of us. So I left the fanboy stuff to everyone else, swearing off that kind of reverence as weak.

I picked Imam Siraj up from the airport for the Grand Opening, and he asked me questions about the itinerary that strongly suggested what changes be made. I made the changes via text immediately. He told me when to pick him up and what he preferred for breakfast, always with the most respectful tone and deference because of my position. I was happy to accommodate.

He gave me advice on navigating some of the challenges I was facing in my leadership. I took detailed notes. Not just what he was saying but how he was saying it, what books he had stacked under his arm, everything.

I was starstruck, I couldn't front.

But can you blame me?

Beyond Black History, Imam **Siraj Wahhaj** is American History. He is Islamic History. He is One of the Tallest Giants in Our Midst.

GIANT PRINCIPLE:

Stand Tall. Nothing can stand against you if the Creator is with you.

Chapter 14:
Nadim Ali

Nadim S. Ali, LPC
Imam, Counselor

Temper is a
physical reaction.

When the temper I inherited from Larry Moore would flare up, my chest would feel like the air was leaving to make way for fire, and my ears would be hot to the touch. I'd have to remind myself to breathe. That temper and humility were my most significant issues growing up. Success in school and sports made me insufferably cocky. If I didn't get my way, I would silently fume.

Like my father, I turned to boxing and fighting as an outlet for my temper. Maybe it was the Sonny Liston in our bloodline, but somehow I could see my opponents' key weaknesses in a street fight in slow motion and had the precision and strength to exploit them. When I landed a signature blow, the "Ooohs!!" from the crowd and the superstar post-fight treatment fed my ego and validated my temper.

But the older I got, the more deadly fighting became. People stopped just taking a whipping. When Farouq died at the shed after someone got beat up and came back spraying bullets at the whole court, it was crystal clear to me: Win a fight and lose your life was a daily tradeoff in the hood.

So I had to figure out how to calm myself down.

Sometimes going to Abu with an issue didn't help. It was hot coal asking the fire how to be cool. But the beauty of a community is the variety of examples available to the kids growing up in it. I needed a cool-headed mentor to help me through my anger issues, and the one who stood out the most was Brother Nadim Ali.

A smooth-talking, even keel poet from Chester, PA, Brother Nadim was as cool as they come. He was the leader of an acapella quartet called the Dawah Ensemble, which doubled as Imam Jamil Al-Amin's sahabah and personal security detail.

His wife Mu'mina was my 6th-grade teacher and had gotten an up-close and personal look at my intelligence and temper when their daughter Asiya beat me out for valedictorian by a few decimals. Sister Mu'mina tells the story about how cocky I got at the end of the year. Brother Nadim chuckled the first time he heard it and didn't miss the chance to offer me some words of advice.

I got the sense that he'd been where I was before.

A licensed professional counselor later chosen to lead Imam Jamil's community, I began to lean on Imam Nadim more and more through the years, including for premarital counseling. If ever I was involved in a conflict, I had a choice; call Abu to be ignited or Imam Nadim to be cooled down. If not for his wisdom, cooler heads would not have prevailed in several intense encounters I have been applauded for handling.

Imam **Nadim Sulaiman Ali** is a Giant in Our Midst.

GIANT PRINCIPLE:

Stay Cool under fire.

Chapter 15:
Adeyinka Mendes

Adeyinka Mendes
Poet, Imam, Historian

"We are not human beings having a
spiritual experience; we are spiritual beings
having a human experience."
~ Pierre Teilhard de Chardin

When I hear this quote, one person comes to mind.

I met Adeyinka Mendes a few names ago. Introduced to me as Sheikh Muhammad Mendes Abdul-Haqq, my ears perked up for obvious reasons. In the Black American Muslim world, sharing a last name does not mean you have an ancestor in common. Most likely, the name was chosen within the last 50 years. But the meanings of names do tend to dictate the paths that we take.

Abdul-Haqq means "Servant of The Truth." Knowing how much carrying that title has shaped me and seeing how humble and sincere this man felt while simply shaking his hands, there was an instant connection that went deeper than having the same great uncle would have.

This man was distinct. There was a light touch to his speech and interpretations. He radiated wisdom that belied his young face. He displayed his beliefs in his actions, smile, and service. When he spoke, whether in intimate gatherings or in front of large crowds, he told stories about the prophets, their companions, and other historical figures in ways that made you wonder if he was there.

Over the years, the world began recognizing his gifts as an orator, teacher, and speaker, and his audiences grew. Constantly soaking up knowledge in his travels and studies, Sheikh Muhammad Mendes Abdul-Haqq became Sheikh Muhammad Adeyinka Mendes as his focus on Black contributions to Islam intensified.

Today, he simply goes by Adeyinka Mendes. But the character of his role model, Muhammad the Prophet, and his unwavering commitment to the truth are ever-present in his leadership and ministry. If that doesn't make a person a Sheikh, I don't know what does.

Suppose ever I begin to doubt we are spiritual beings having a human experience. In that case, I'll think about how much meeting

Adeyinka Mendes reminded me of the time a man dressed in all white approached Muhammad and asked him about Islam, faith, the final hour, and its signs.

Those who know, know.
Adeyinka Mendes is Black History in the Making.
He is a Giant in Our Midst.

GIANT PRINCIPLE:

Embody Wisdom, Serenity, and Greatness.
Make people wonder if you are
connected to a higher power.

Chapter 16:
Sulaimaan Hamed

"Welcome home."

Nearly a decade since I moved from Atlanta, these words have grown in meaning with each passing year. When I visit my hometown, I hear them from the leader of the largest Muslim community in Atlanta on its busiest day without fail.

Atlanta Masjid of Al-Islam is one of the flagship communities in the late Imam W.D. Mohammed's national network. On Fridays, one thousand people congregate there to hear Imam Sulaimaan Hamed speak.

He addresses them with an ever-present gleam in his eye. The gleam says he thoroughly enjoys sharing what he has studied with the people he loves. It says that he sees humor or irony in almost every situation. That underneath the garb, the years of learning, and the title, it isn't lost on him that he's still a young man from Oakland who has beaten the odds to be in a position to lead and speak to a thousand plus people every week.

Sulaimaan speaks in the conversational tone of a young uncle at a family reunion. He's wise and learned enough to appeal to the elders in the family with stories of yesteryear, cool enough to be able to translate them into modern terms for the youngsters, and funny enough to bring everyone together laughing about the moral of the story — even if it's exposing a sore spot.

After Jummah, everyone files out to the lobby and the bazaar outside while Sulaimaan goes to his office. But he leaves the door wide open. You don't need an appointment to see him at this time, so plenty of people come in just to speak, others bring food or gifts, and some bring their laundry list of complaints. Sulaimaan gives them all his undivided attention and nods with the gleam still in his eye.

But somehow, he still spots little old me in the lobby the few times a year that I'm in town, makes his way through the crowd to shake my hand, look me in the eye and say, "welcome home."

He has taught me more about leadership with this simple, consistent gesture than years of schooling ever could.

Sulaimaan Hamed is Black History in the Making.
He is a Giant in Our Midst.

GIANT PRINCIPLE:

Be Humble. Let your passion illuminate your community, and accept criticism with a twinkle in your eye.

Chapter 17:
Noor Jihan

Noor Jihan
Physician, En...

Black
History
In the Making

"You know you're the new
Clara Luper, right?"

East End Girls and West End Boys

Although only a 10-minute drive separates the West End and Atlanta Masjids off of I-20, they couldn't have been further apart in their approach to Islam in the 1970s, 80s, and 90s.

Like the Tablighi Jamat, Imam Jamil Al-Amin's West End community is an offshoot of the Darul Islam Movement. Darul Islam, or "The Dar," was more apt to accept rigid interpretations of the Prophet Muhammad's words and actions, a literal translation of the Qur'an, and avoid non-Islamic influences. As I discussed in Abu and Abdullah Rabbani's chapters, this often translates into hostility toward American social, political, religious, and educational institutions.

The Atlanta Masjid follows the teachings of Imam Warith Deen Mohammed, who brought thousands of Muslims from his father Elijah Muhammad's Nation of Islam into al-Islam Proper. The Warith Deen or "WD" community emphasized learning to read and interpret the Qur'an for yourself and using it to propel community life forward.

Whereas the Dar's emphasis on discipline, militancy, and rote learning attracted bold, wild types who needed order, WD's cerebral "man means mind" and "words make people" mantras attracted more academic, free-thinking types. Therefore, Dar communities like the West End were largely populated by ex-convicts who took their shahada in prison and credited Islam with their reform. And WD communities were home to more college graduates who credited Islam with freeing their minds.

A Black American Muslim man in a thobe, kamees, or turban in Atlanta likely belonged to the West End community or one of its offshoots. Women from these communities mostly wore dark, loose-fitting jilbabs and khimars draped in the front, covering their necks and chest. Some women wore niqab, which cover everything but the eyes.

On Fridays for Jumuah, the weekly congregational sermon and prayer, men outnumbered women 75 to 25 and were separated by a wall.

A Black American Muslim man in a suit and a shaved or trimmed beard in Atlanta likely belonged to the Atlanta Masjid community or its offshoot. Most women wear free-flowing colorful clothes and a khimar tied into a bun, wrapped around their hair, or draped for prayer only. At Jumuah, they all gather in one large room with men in front and women in the back. The women seem to outnumber the men by 400 to 350.

Of course, there were exceptions in each community.

As soon as I became old enough to ride the bus to Jumuah, I started going to Atlanta Masjid a couple of times a month. I was always turned off by the notion that a man from Pakistan, India, or Yemen centuries before me, but centuries after the Prophet Muhammad, was somehow more qualified to interpret how Islam was to be applied to my life in America than a scholarly person living in America. On the one hand, Imam Jamil would often say 'The Qur'an isn't history; it's news." But on the other hand, my youthful, probing questions were often met with responses that made curiosity feel haram.

I liked going to Atlanta Masjid because being young, Black, American, and inquisitive felt halal there.

Us West End boys and our street edge were a little risque and taboo for the colorful Atlanta Masjid girls surrounded by buttoned-up East Atlanta boys. And the West End girls were too close for comfort, more like first cousins than wives in our eyes. So cross-community interest was mutual. I knew my wife was going to come from Atlanta Masjid.

Allah Made Me Funny

By 2008, I was a 26-year-old Muslim bachelor with a clock ticking loudly in my head.

After all, marriage was half of the way of life I was pursuing. I wanted to be a leader in the community and didn't want to be 50 at my first child's high school graduation. Plus, being single at 26 in the Muslim community is cause for a lot of raised eyebrows and gossip. So I did plenty of homework on potential wife types at Muslim social events and on Facebook between work, schoolwork, and working out.

That fall, I ran into a Sister I had never seen before at two events, back to back.

The first event was a showing of the 'Kings of Comedy' styled special 'Allah Made Me Funny' at the Midtown Art Cinema. Hollywood's only acknowledgment of Black American Muslim existence for years was stiff, one-dimensional characters with kufis who only exist to spoil the hero's fun. Muslims were only known for what we couldn't do.

"See, I'm African American and Muslim.
The United States is scared of two things:
Black people… and Muslims.
I got the best of both worlds!"

For creatives like myself, Preacher Moss saying this on the big screen was groundbreaking and inspirational.

After the show, everyone was buzzing after seeing their stories on the big screen and in a great mood. But, even from a respectful distance, I noticed a poised, modest, self-assured, outspoken Sister who resembled the 'A Different World' version of Jada Pinkett in a headwrap. She was chatting with people I knew, but I had never seen her. So I put myself in her walking path to say "Saaalaikum" in a way that said, "I see you."

She returned the greeting and kept moving to her silver Honda Civic with a pink and green AKA tag on the back.

I was with Ayyub and Ndola. When I returned to the car, I asked Ndola, "Who was that Sister in the yellow??"

Ndola replied, "Who, the doctor? I think her name is Jihan. She's cool."

I mumbled some stuff out loud that only my brother could decipher. Ndola rolled her eyes and laughed. I went home and added "Jihan the Doctor" to my prospective wives spreadsheet.

Yes, I had a spreadsheet.

The Spreadsheet

After my failed first marriage, where I went completely off of convenience, appearance, and the arrogant assumption that I could make any relationship work if I wanted to, I was taking the opposite approach this time. Informed by my previous relationships and present goals, I was looking for someone who would complement me more than they complimented me. So I put the names of Sisters I could see completing my present and future versions on the spreadsheet. Some were already friends of mine, and others I had never said a word to in my life but gave me vibes that made me believe they would like me if they got to know me.

The criteria of the list were weighted as follows.

1. On her Deen - she had to be trying her best to be a good Muslim. I was as imperfect as they came, but I was an imperfect *Muslim*. So I needed a wife who was an imperfect Muslimah with whom I could compare notes. Surely, our imperfections would not all match, nor would our approaches to overcome them. Together, we would help the other cross off flaws. But I would rather marry a Christian Bible thumper than a Muslimah who ignores the Qur'an.

2. Stable family - My family was spread out all over the country, somewhat fractured and distant. I spoke with Umi, Najwa, and Yaseen weekly at best and Abu, Sumayyah, and Kaleema monthly at best. I had only met my sister Amira twice in my entire life. None of us had beef. We were just content with knowing the others were alive and well, and didn't feel a need to check in regularly. I wanted a closer experience for my children. So I wanted to marry someone from a family I could learn closeness from and my children to have a tight group of aunties, uncles, and grandparents on one side of their tree.

3. Looks - From my experience, the prettiest women were often the craziest ones. Constant attention, compliments, and pressure from men from an early age seemed to affect women negatively if not balanced by other qualities. So she didn't have to be jaw-dropping gorgeous, per se. But also, from my experience, attraction is a significant floor-raiser in a relationship. It's hard to stay mad at someone who speeds up your heartbeat just by looking how they be looking. And the attention they receive inspires you to do things to remain The One for them. Plus, if you have beautiful women in your family or past, you're doing your wife a disservice if she can't hold her own, looks-wise, in an encounter with one of them.

4. Conversation - I didn't realize how much I played Madden 2004 during my first marriage until I was preparing for the 2024 draft. The lack of conversation between Zakiya and me was torture, and Madden was my way of avoiding it. It didn't seem fair that I had to cut off running conversations with my friends for a wife who couldn't stimulate me mentally. It was like someone having a Lamborghini in the driveway that they couldn't drive but got mad at others for noticing or wanting to take it for a spin. Despite the player rumors, I never approached a stranger intending to get her phone number. I didn't have game or pick-up lines. My primary means of developing and maintaining relationships was always conversation.

5. Feeling Me - I'm a big fan of myself, so how could I be married to someone who didn't share that love?

6. Ambition - Especially as it relates to Black women, this term has morphed over the past few decades. It used to mean having a plan and desiring to get an education to support and stimulate an educated man and develop his children. Now it means getting an education to build generational wealth for yourself and not have to depend on a man. I was interested in a mixture of both. I wanted someone who, like me, did not believe in the "two footprints became one" approach to marriage. I had my mission and preferred her to have one of her own. That way, I could help her accomplish her goals and vice versa.

7. Attachments - Exes she isn't quite over, children, and substantial debt matter when choosing a life partner. It was more of a tie-breaker than a deal-breaker for me because I was bringing a carry-on bag of my own to the journey.

8. Background Proximity - The ideal candidate would be close enough not to have to explain my entire lifestyle but far enough not to think of her like my sister.

9. Strength of Voice - After my experience with Zakiya, I knew I wanted a partner, not a servant. I appreciate a woman keeping me in line with my stated goals, regardless of how that may look or sound. This criterion is part of number one when you think about it. The Prophet Muhammad married and often took counsel from strong-minded women.

"Jihan the AKA" got high marks in 1, 3, 6, and 8 just from our brief encounter. I needed to evaluate the rest ASAP.

Let it Burn

The second event was at an Eid al-Fitr game night for young adults. The event's promoters were Inshirah Jihad from the West End and Aseelah Rashid from the Atlanta Masjid – the best promoters from each respective community. So I knew the event would be well-planned and well-attended by women on my spreadsheet. They held it at Ikhlas, a staple among Atlanta seafood restaurants. But Ikhlas wasn't known as an event center, so I knew it would be an intimate gathering. I needed to look and smell my best.

On the event day, I got a fresh haircut, took an afternoon shower, moisturized with cocoa butter, brushed my teeth, put on some blue jeans, a white v-neck t-shirt underneath a blue button-up, dark brown corduroy jacket, and brown Italian boots. I sprayed Jean Paul Gaultier cologne once into my right wrist, rubbed it against my left, and used both wrists to spread the scent down both sides of my neck and shirt. Then, ready in enough time to get there when the doors opened, I made Asr prayer and browsed the internet for 30 minutes. My entrance needed an audience, and arriving on time did not provide one. I figured Ms. AKA would get there on time.

When I walked inside Ikhlas, I flipped my Prom King switch, and the quiet introvert stayed outside. The night's objective was to see and be seen, so the response to every invitation and every challenge was yes. I saw Jihan in the crowd, but by no means did that mean I would go holler at her. The objective was to ensure she saw me and, more importantly, how other women saw me. Women like men who other women want.

Khalfani was in the building, and I told him, "No no's tonight, bruh. It's showtime. Let's have some fun!"

Khalfani grinned and nodded his approval, saying, "I'm down, akh let's go!"

When the room was sufficiently packed, Inshirah and Aseelah took the stage and announced the first competition. It would be a group of Sisters vs. a group of Brothers, and the game was 'Finish the Lyrics.'

"Do we have any volunteers for the Brothers?" Aseelah asked, scanning the room full of too-cool Brothers vigorously shaking their heads no. When her eyes got to me, she saw my left hand raised high and my right elbow nudging Khalfani, who raised his hand too, cheesing. Then, seeing us reserved, former pretty boy thug types raise our hands, three other brothers raised their hands, and we had our squad.

After the Sisters struggled through a Beyonce song and a Mariah Carey song, I led my group on stage and grabbed the microphone. Inshirah repeated the rules of the game, reminding us that the Sisters knew the lyrics to their songs, so we needed to nail both of ours to stay alive.

I smiled at the crowd, then said, "We ready, Inshirah! We're gonna make it sound good, though."

I stared at the group of Sisters who had just performed, and the crowd burst into laughter. It was the first time I'd seen Jihan laugh.

"If I keep her laughing and rolling her eyes all night, it's a wrap," I thought.

Inshirah kicked it to the DJ, and Khalfani took her mic. Confident that our combined encyclopedic knowledge of hip-hop and R&B would not let us down, we listened closely to what the DJ played. But everyone's eyebrows raised when we heard a near whisper from the speakers.

Recognizing the song as Usher's 'Burn,' the crowd began taunting me for my overconfidence, led by the group of Sisters who had just sung.

Khalfani tried to find takers for his microphone, not wanting to tackle Usher's range in front of the crowd. But, unfortunately, no one accepted, and it looked like the Brothers were going to fold before we even began.

Frowning at my bandmates and making a motion that said I Got This, I channeled my inner David Ruffin, moving to the very front and center of the stage as I belted out the lyrics, cadence for cadence with Usher.

I close my eyes, bend slightly at the waist, and place my right hand over my heart. The crowd falls over themselves in laughter and joins me.

My backup singers turn into hypemen, ad-libbing and gassing me up to finish the lyrics by hitting the upcoming high notes they were all afraid of.

The crowd erupts, egging me on, and I continue into a cracking falsetto, digging deep to push out the notes. Then, finally, the DJ kills the music, and only my voice remains to finish the lyrics.

The room goes crazy.

I see members of the list interacting and can't help but zero in on the smiling and clapping Jihan near the front row.

I mentally add number 5, "Feeling Me," to her name on the spreadsheet.

The lyrics I just sang may as well have been addressed to every other woman on the list in the room.

Aseelah came on stage and said, "Okay! Looks like someone is trying to find a wife tonight! We see you, Brother Masood!"

I made an incredulous "Who me?" gesture.

Aseelah continued, "That was nice, but remember, the sisters finished the lyrics to two songs. So Brothers, yall have to get this next song, or ALL THAT would be for nothing."

Aseelah gave the DJ the cue to start the next song. It had rolling drums, trumpets and whistles, and a smooth bassline that I recognized. It belonged to Outkast's 'Morris Brown.' Not the rapping part at the beginning of the song, but the singing part, which would be a piece of cake after Usher. So I relaxed and focused on showing that I could carry a tune and control the crowd.

The DJ killed the music, and I led the chorus.

I waved in Jihan's direction and laughed my way off stage to a rousing applause.

The entire performance was me telling the other women in the room to let the idea of 'us' burn while saying hey to a future with Jihan.

What they say about The One is true –
when you know, you know.

That moment when you see your entire future in a headwrap

Over the next few weeks, Jihan and I struck up a back-and-forth online, feeling each other out by commenting on each other's posts and periodic direct messages. Then, finally, we started talking on the phone at the end of December 2008 and spending time together nearly every day toward the middle of January 2009. She was an excellent conversationalist and came from a very close-knit family, so she was number one with a bullet on my spreadsheet by that time.

Noor Jihan means light of the world, and it couldn't have been more appropriate given how she brightened up my regimented life. But it wasn't all butterflies and heart eyes. I was enamored by her posture, seriousness, modesty, and ambition.

She was probably just impressed by my audacity. Plus, only a few Brothers were checking for confident, pretty Sisters with double degrees. The market was better for the Zakiyas of the world.

Either way, I started talking her up to my mother and brothers.

"She doesn't feel random or like a homegirl or a Facebook friend. And I don't want to see her with anyone else… So I think that means she's a wife."

They all replied, "well, go get her then."

But the world wasn't shy about letting us know we didn't match on paper. My detractors knew everything you now know about my adolescent years, minus the context. So to them, I was just a thugged-out player and former high school dropout from the West End with no degree. And she was one of the crown jewels of the Atlanta Masjid community. She was a Pediatrician in residency after graduating from Morehouse School of Medicine, and I was a hotel manager. Someone hacked my computer and sent Jihan photos of Suki and me, saying something about her being my second choice. They sent anonymous letters to Jihan's parents and to the leadership at Atlanta Masjid attacking my character. But those efforts only made Jihan and me closer.

"If you're so bad, why are they mad you're not marrying them?" she asked.

Black Love in America

I typed a text to this girl I used to see.
Told her that I found this cutie pie with whom
I want to be. And I apologize if this message
gets you down. Then I CC'd every girl that I'd
see-see round town. ~ André Benjamin.

After I made it clear to everyone that I was pursuing Jihan, we spent time bonding and getting to know one another each evening for six weeks straight. We'd put our phones down each night after work and take turns reading each other a chapter out of The Secret Life of Bees. Then we watched the film when we were done.

Nothing was beneath me as long as I got to know Jihan. One night I sat Indian style on her living room floor, helping her paint small benches pink and green so she could gift them to her AKA Neos. I learned then that her line sisters were like her real sisters and that if she was stuck up, it wasn't her Alpha Kappa Alpha side, but the Spelman side.

We discussed everything vital to us, from Islam to politics, basketball to firearms. Thanks to a month-long ER rotation, she was traumatized by the damage she saw bullets cause to human bodies. So she was adamantly opposed to having guns in the house. I had owned at least one gun since I was 15 and went to the range regularly. One evening, the issue resolved itself when she returned home to a wide-open front door. She ran back to her car and called me to ask if I could come over and ensure no one was inside her condo. I said of course. Before we hung up, she said quietly, "Can you bring your gun?"

Like I was going to show up to confront a home invader without it.

There was no one there, but I cleared each room like an ATF agent before announcing it was safe for her to enter.

January 20, 2008, was a pivotal and memorable day for our budding courtship. Despite principles that make me suspicious of anyone inhabiting the Oval Office, how First Lady Michelle Obama complemented President Barack at his inauguration was inspirational. Two poised and accomplished Black people supporting and loving each other on the world stage was a seminal moment for Black love in America, and it was contagious. Jihan and I watched it together in awe.

Neither of us celebrated Valentine's Day, but we agreed to make mix cds for each other and exchange them on February 15th. The one song both of us chose was Truly, Madly, Deeply by Savage Garden. My New Mexico and her Oklahoma childhoods were aligning.

I told her, "I would marry you right now if it wasn't crazy."

"Shoot... don't play with me, Brother," she replied.

"Scratch that, I'm going to marry you. I need to meet your father first, though. Hook it up." I said matter of factly.

Not the most romantic proposal story, but I was channeling my inner Brother Abdullah by assuming the sale.

A few weeks later, on a trip to Memphis, I met her family, community elders from her hometown of Oklahoma City, and a key Spelman sister and got the ok. We then completed premarital counseling with Imam Nadim. Then Noor Jihan and I got married in a small, let's-not-live-in-sin ceremony officiated by Imam Nadim and attended by Umi, Abu Shaka, Sumayyah, and Jihan's parents. Our courtship was thorough and intentional and only took 5 and a half months.

GIANT PRINCIPLE:

Never let someone tell you they need a few years to figure out if they really want you. They know within a few encounters. Their real dilemma is whether they can go without what they use you for.

Access to new levels of Giants

After getting married for a second time by Imam Sulaimaan Hamed in front of friends and family in September, we made it super official by filing for a marriage license with the state of Georgia. The event was attended by people from all walks of life, many of whom would never cross paths if not for our union.

It was a beautiful event, complete with Qur'an recitation, Imam jokes about my waves, four Christian grandparents in a Masjid, 15 siblings, Bobbi's mother, Ms. Loraine, thugs in suits, AKA's in hijab, photography by Karina, and me serenading Jihan at the reception with another rendition of "Morris Brown" with the help of a live band called Gritz and Jellybutter.

Though Jihan and I knew we complemented each other well, the wedding was our first taste of how our different backgrounds manifested in social settings.

A Seat at the Table

In the months and years to come, Jihan and I were invited to attend galas, banquets, fundraisers and the weddings of several of our friends and family members. I knew how to rock a suit and could be the star of any conversation at any table, so I would get the early nod approval from Jihan's Spelhouse friends and their spouses at these types of events. When the lawyers, judges, doctors, and politicians who were Jihan's classmates started to like me, they would naturally inquire, "Did you go to Morehouse?" in a way that suggested they were surprised they didn't remember me. I would say no, and then things would get awkward from there.

"Oh, ok. Where did you graduate from?"

"I didn't go to college, out of high school. I started a business with my friends instead."

"Ok nice. What's the business?"

"It was a hip-hop clothing company. I'm not there anymore, though."

"Oh... So what do you do now?"

"I run a hotel and do some freelance copywriting on the side."

"Oh, cool! I have an idea for a device that helps..."

"Not copyrighting, copy W-R-I-T-I-N-G. Like ads, direct mail, slogans, etc."

"Oh. Ok..."

A similar dynamic would form during discussions with the Coca-Cola executives and Senators who stayed at my hotels. They'd bring complex situations from their 1%er jobs to me during our chats in the lobby, and I never missed a beat, even offering solutions that made more sense than any of the MBAs on their team could come up with. They would then ask questions that said everything but "Why the hell are *you* working *here*?"

One Senator gave me his U.S. Senate lapel pin and said, "I hope to see you on that floor with me one day. You certainly have the chops for it."

As confident, well-read, and experienced as I was, those interactions bothered me. These people were my intellectual equals at best, and many had a fraction of my social skills. But they made 3 to 10 times the money I did, primarily because they chose their careers early, got the degrees for it, and I didn't.

Jihan never pressured me to go back to school. She pointed to all of the things I did for my team and the promotions I was in line for at work, the work I was doing with at-risk youth, and how well I took care of her as reasons she loved me just the way I was.

Scared Money Don't Make None
But being in rooms with money and power
changes the conversation in your head.

Networking with successful people changes how and what you study and the type of people you model your behavior after. When you know someone who has accomplished what you previously only read about or saw on TV, their level of success no longer seems magical, lucky, or unattainable. One thing I picked up in conversations with this new level of Giants was that pressure from commitments creates a sense of responsibility.

I already knew and believed it from watching Shobe shoot dice on Atwood and hearing, "Scared money don't make none!" from the side bettors. From being there when Ebro and Ahmad would take hundreds of thousands of dollars in orders with no inventory or supplies on hand and deliver. I learned the extent of my conviction in this principle when I could not stop debating with a business professor at a scam college after he told my classmates that taking an order when you did not have the inventory on hand was unethical.

But wealthy people take it further. They love spending OPM - other people's money. Loans, grants, credit lines, tax breaks, whatever they must do to make themselves accountable for delivering on a promise. That kind of pressure makes diamonds. After a self-assessment, I found myself guilty of not taking enough risks and playing life too safe. It worked when the goal was to survive. But not now, that the goal was to thrive and provide.

Oklahoma

Familiarity and comfort can insulate you from this frigid world, but they can also pigeonhole you and lull you to sleep. By 30, my faith was on an upswing. I had made significant personal and professional strides, married a fantastic woman and brought twins into the world. The leaders I respected, respected me, but I was ready for everyone around me to see me for who I was, not who I used to be. So I began weighing the pros and cons of changing scenery to a place where everyone was forced to evaluate me on merit. As I discussed in Zak's chapter, hijrah is essential to Islamic history and application. Uprooting your life and relocating requires immense faith.

I told Jihan I wanted to attend a four-year university, learn more about how money works, and get a Business degree. After some discussion, we determined the best way to do that would be for us to move to Oklahoma, where her family could help us with our 1-year-old twins, and our cost of living would be cheaper. So, in the summer of 2012,

Yaseen and I went to Oklahoma City to renovate one of Jihan's father's rental properties. A month later, I went back to Atlanta, and our family of four made hijrah to one of the rest stops on the Abdul-Haqq migration from Abiquiu to Atlanta 20 years prior.

I continued in hotel management in Oklahoma until May 20, 2013. That day, a mile-wide EF5 tornado formed two miles from my hotel, went on a 39-minute, 17-mile rampage to the city of Moore, and ground everything in its path. We spent part of that night in my sister-in-law Aquilah's underground tornado shelter. For much of the next two days - which I had off from work - we were sans electricity, cleaning up debris and detraumatizing the twins.

When I returned to work, my manager was passive-aggressive because I didn't come in on my days off. She gave me a list of duties, including taking out all trash in the hotel. I asked why I would do that when the maintenance and housekeeping managers reported to me. She responded with something that sounded racist, so I quit.

Jihan implored me not to get another job and just go to school full-time so that I could finish faster. She argued that our expenses were low, and she made enough to cover whatever she needed. I agreed to start taking a full class load, but not to be sponsored by my wife. The internet sheikhs and single marriage experts would never let me hear the end of it. Instead, I worked nights and drove Uber part-time while taking five classes a semester. I also figured out other ways to add value to Jihan's life.

Jihan was frustrated with the lack of social or educational activity at the masjid she grew up in, so I volunteered to teach a Qur'an class, coordinate Ramadan and Eid activities, and join the board. For her 33rd birthday, she asked me to give the Khutbah (sermon), so I finally accepted the Imam's request and did it. He decided to make me a regular on the first Fridays, and I developed into a good speaker. Later, I joined the board of the Council on American - Islamic Relations Oklahoma chapter. These moves positioned me to hit the ground running once I completed my Business Law degree. I could leverage my relationships, public speaking experience, and proximity to power into a political or commercial real estate career.

Now Chairman of the Masjid and CAIR Oklahoma, I spearhead a $7 million commercial real estate project that is bringing a community center, six new businesses, and affordable housing to the Eastside of Oklahoma City - the Black side of town that was redlined out of prosperity over the years despite being in the shadow of the Governor's mansion and the state capitol building.

Aftermath

"You know you're the new Clara Luper, right?"

Our sweet nothings are something else.

In Oklahoma, the gold standard for community organizing and activism is Ms. Clara Luper, a teacher and Civil Rights leader best remembered for organizing some of the nation's earliest youth sit-ins with some of her students. Well into her old age, Ms. Luper continued to teach young men and women the power of the vote, assembly, and speech through the Oklahoma City Youth Council. Youth Council members were trained to be activists, regardless of their professions.

Noor-Jihan Ahmad was one of those young women.

In 2015, after becoming disenchanted with the bottom-line-driven approach of her employer, we decided to open Peace of Mind Pediatrics, where Noor Jihan could practice medicine her way. As owner and Chief Medical officer, Noor Jihan takes a hands-on, holistic approach to medicine that does more than push pharmaceuticals.

Much like her mentor Ms. Luper, Noor Jihan is an educator of youth and a constant inspiration to all she encounters. She is every bit of the world changer that Ms. Luper and her mother molded her to be, with a heart that feels joy, sadness, and pain for people she has never met and a mind that never stops thinking of solutions. My job is to download those ideas, sort them out, pick which ones are most realistic and help her think of ways to make them work within our schedules.

This system has led us to parenthood, successful serial entrepreneurship, and more community service than I ever dreamed of. Noor Jihan now uses her platform as a loudspeaker for the underserved.

I'm just honored to be the first one she encounters each day.

Dr. Noor Jihan Abdul-Haqq is Black History in the Making.
She is a Giant in Our Midst.

GIANT PRINCIPLE:

Shine Your Light on the world.
Serve the underserved and light up
every room with your smile.

PART III:
The Inspirational

Unfaithful

Her name is Iman. When we were young, I couldn't imagine anything coming between us. She was with me when the training wheels finally came off my royal blue Huffy, and she even stayed around to watch me attempt to conquer the steepest hill in town on my first ride.

She came to all of my spelling bees, basketball games, and school plays and made me feel invincible when she entered the room. I didn't even have to look around; I knew when she was there. She was only as old as I was, but I got the sense that she'd been around for a while longer. Call it a hunch or a superstition. But all I know is that she made me feel like the world was my own set, and I was the writer, director, and star. Anything I dreamt of was possible with her, and I was convinced that nothing was possible without her. Yet, she persisted:

"One day we won't be as close, Masood," she would whisper into my subconscious. "There will be others who come along and hate what we have. They will openly rail against it even."

It was ironic to me that someone as steady and inspirational as she was seemingly so paranoid and insecure.

But in time, her words rang truer and truer. Once adolescence came, there were so many more girls. Girls with pretty teeth and manicured fingernails. Girls with…well, pretty girls. Intellectually stimulating girls. And these girls made sure I knew they were there. Every time

I looked around, there were more pretty smiles, and those manicured fingers were reaching out to me and getting closer and closer by the day. I knew I shouldn't let them, but some of me eventually felt I deserved the attention. Then the rest of me decided that I needed the attention.

That's when Iman got sick and had to move away.

Seasons cycled, and the pretty girls turned into beautiful women. The intellectually stimulating ones turned into successful women. Conquered hills became conquered mountains, and my sense of entitlement erupted into full-scale solipsism — so much so that I didn't even remember Iman at all.

I was young, ambitious, and outwardly attractive but inwardly as unstable as that first bike ride. But this time, something besides just the training wheels was missing. Iman was missing. So I experienced something I had never experienced before…

I fell.

I fell spectacularly.

Face first, I fell from the ranks of the solipsistic to those of the desolate. The silver specks that highlighted my hair multiplied, and my left eye swelled shut from the impact of my fall. Outside of myself, my point of view was now panoramic, and as I observed myself from above, I was ashamed.

I mean, who was I to be casually brilliant, outwardly attractive, and talented? I thought of the many hearts I stepped on, the pish-tosh nonchalance that came to embody my social being, and the relative ease with which I went about being above average.

I knew that if it was easy for me to be above average, I should be striving for greatness.

I feel like a boxer with the best promoter and the worst trainer, and they are both me. Here I am under these bright lights versus life, with everyone watching. My robe is fit for a king. My entrance was grand, and my warm-up punches were crisp and intimidating. Sans robe, I appear to be in tip-top shape, and onlookers that know nothing of either opponent picked me based on appearance alone. But it's only the second round, and I'm already out of breath. I've gone to the clutch. The crowd is growing antsy, and between blows to the nose and work on my body, I can hear a smattering of boos...

So I studied greatness and realized it is a learned behavior. I gained an understanding of why and how it is unattainable without dedication, focus, and commitment. I conducted an internal audit and realized that I was flagrantly low on all three. No wonder my life was in shambles. No wonder making prayer was such a chore. No wonder I was... in a word, unfaithful.

Damn.

Was it too late to change?

I look up at the blurry clock with my unswollen eye and tell myself that 1 minute isn't bad.

I'll get it together. I was a golden gloves champ! Fox ran specials on me at ages 16 and 21 that aired from Atlanta to Las Vegas! I trained in the high altitude of the Rocky Mountains and in the sweltering Southeastern humidity, sparring in the southwestern streets of Atlanta! 60 seconds. I show my bloodied mouthpiece at the irony. 60 seconds in 1 minute. That could be the title of my life story. A jack of all trades and a master of none. Never first, but always in the running. Record-breaking futility. 60 2nds in one minute. Ha! I laugh as I absorb another crushing blow to the jaw. My head snaps to the side of the ring my friends were on. Their row is empty. I tell my arms to swing, but my legs intercept the order and swing from underneath me. I'm going down. I wonder how many seconds are left as I brace myself for impact. The colors are all running together, but one image stands out clearly from the kaleidoscope-like landscape. It's a face, a familiar face. I crash into the rock-hard canvas. Rock bottom. I close my eyes. Then a smile creeps up from my heart, up into my eyes. I remember that face now. It was Iman. She had come back just when life had started to kick my butt...

Fade to black.

It's been a while now since I retired from the game. Sure, the sweet science still permeates a thought or ten every now and then, but I'm done with it for good. I still walk proudly like the fighter I once was — shoulders squared, head high, and eyes dancing about my surroundings. My body carries with it the aches and the scars from wounds that did not close until lessons seeped in, and my name carries with it the notoriety and stigma of a man who has conquered and been conquered on the grandest of stages. But no longer do I carry with me the cumbersome burden of proof. I do not feel the need to measure my merits against those of other men. I don't have to back up any self-afflicted hype. No promoter, no trainer, no friends, no foes, I am content with honing my skills under the watchful eyes of time and its creator...

Since I lifted myself off the floor and picked up the pieces of my life that were left, Iman has been with me. It wasn't glorious or triumphant, and it definitely wasn't romantic. At first, it felt more like a mother grabbing her son by the ear and walking him out of the principal's office after she finds out he has been failing his best subject. But we've made considerable progress since that day. I don't think she forgot about how I played her for all those girls back in the day, but she doesn't rub it in. She just seems intent on not letting it happen again. She said once, "Breaking female hearts is like chicken pox, Masood. You better have gotten it out of your system when you were young because if it happens when you're grown, it can be deadly." She's good with analogies like that. She understands what I need to hear and what I need to see.

She's got me focused again. I'm finally dedicated to singular targets instead of a series of quick-moving ones that will only hurt me in the long run. I'm prioritizing and attacking, repeating the same formulas for success until they become second nature. I can't even tell you the last time I lost something because, with her, there are no wins and losses, just opportunities. Either an opportunity to succeed or an opportunity to find out what to improve. I have strong Faith in my new target-based approach.

My breathing is steady. My eyes trained forward in a trance-like glare, and all of my senses are heightened. The pit-pat of my heart is faint, even soothing. But it is all I hear and serves as the rhythm to which I time my movements. I raise my bow with my locked left arm, slowly tracing a line from my left foot to my target. With my right, I set and draw my arrow back toward my clenched jaw in one seamless motion, never breaking my now icy glare. It's just me and the target now. When I feel the resistance of the bowstrings course through my shoulders and back, I stop breathing. When all movement is stifled, my right hand relaxes, instinctively releasing the string and propelling my arrow through the air with enough velocity to kill a bull. I watch it slice through the air like a guided missile, my body rigidly set in the same stance from which I released it. I'm confident that I'll hit my target but prepared to repeat the process as many times as needed to get it right. The whistling sound of the arrow cutting air is interrupted by a sharp THWAP!

Bulls Eye. Thank God for Iman.

Iman means faith in Arabic.

A lack of tangible proof is a requirement of faith.

Faith is a requirement for inspiration.

The people in this section are the ones who completed my reform by continously inspiring me to be a better version of myself. Most of them were the ones featured in the series, so they are shorter, but no less impactful.

Chapter 18:
Ayyub Abdush-Shakur

The Shakurs
Serial Entrepreneurs

When Abu Shaka Abdush-Shakur married
my mother in 1997, he made it clear that it made
their children - Shaka, Ibrahim, Ayyub, Taharah,
Shakeelah, Larney, Kaleema, Sumayyah, Yaseen,
Me, and Najwa - family. Not steps, just family.

Taharah was best friends with Onida Balli, so I knew her from Atwood Street. Ibrahim would make a cameo over there every now and then too. But I was closest with Ayyub from our affiliation with the Adiyats, a recreational basketball team founded by Imam Jamil that Abu Shaka played on for years before becoming its coach. Ayyub was only 10 months younger than me, so we bonded over basketball at Riyaadahs, the Shed, and at family functions.

A pure shooter who was immaculate with his word, Ayyub was known for being trustworthy and consistent, on and off the court.

When Ayyub went off to college in 2001, I was in full swing with R. World and 4Zero4 Sports. While at school, Ayyub would beam when he saw his classmates wearing the A-Town shirts, but he noticed they were all wearing either the red and blue on white or black and white on grey designs. Knowing we had far more colorways than that, Ayyub approached me about getting some shirts on consignment so he could make some money at school. Of course, I said yes.

Each weekend, Ayyub would return with the money for the shirts and re-up with another couple of dozen. He would hang out with me at the store, observe how I managed the business, and express how inspirational I was to him. That was reformational because knowing he looked up to me made me not want to let him down.

The Getaway

Through his side-view mirror, Ayyub Abdush-Shakur sees Yaseen flying out of the store in a full sprint toward him, with two plainclothes detectives on his trail.

Instinctively, Ayyub turns the key to his not-so-trusty white Nissan Maxima, hoping it doesn't let Yaseen down. After a little hesitation, the car starts, and Ayyub unlocks the doors. But when he looks to the passenger side awaiting his brother's entry, he's startled by a banging on the hood and Yaseen shouting, "GO GO GO GO GO!!!"

Yaseen is spread eagle face down on the hood of the car, gripping the top near the windshield wipers. A wide-eyed Ayyub obliges and peels off into daytime traffic on Cascade Road, with Yaseen hanging on for dear life and the unmarked cars disappearing in the rearview.

How did a good kid like Ayyub, who had never been in trouble his entire life, end up in this predicament? Loyalty, dedication, and a mean competitive spirit.

When the RIAA, FBI, and City of Atlanta waged war against people who sold mixtapes in 2006, it made Yaseen's Royal Brothers CD stand as a public enemy. Ayyub had agreed to take his brother to re-up on the product he sold to make a living off the grid. They had no idea they were walking into a sting operation.

Ayyub's loyalty to his family and dedication to the mission he had set out to accomplish made him hit the gas. His competitive spirit made him figure out how to ditch the Feds in a hooptie with a grown man on his hood.

Thankfully, Ayyub retired as a getaway driver 1-0.

The next year, Ayyub married his childhood crush, Ndola, and her presence meant that Ayyub would not be available for any more shenanigans. Ndola was always a determined, no-nonsense type of young lady. When she came around, she had the presence of an elder, and everyone straightened up a little bit. Their personalities were a perfect match. After becoming parents the following year, when Aziza was born, "Ubi and Ndo" became a standard for many other young people in the community looking to start families. Since then, they have added Jalila and Sara, and their enterprise has only expanded.

With Ndola navigating and Ayyub at the wheel, Ndola has become a scholar, teacher, award-winning baker, and podcaster, Aziza is an emerging fashion designer, and the girls' skin and beauty line JAS has gained international acclaim, landing a grant from Daymond John and a contract with Francesca's.

How does **Ayyub** keep the pedal to the floor while supporting so many enterprising young women? Loyalty, dedication, and a mean competitive spirit.

GIANT PRINCIPLE:

Compete to be consistently good and trustworthy.

Chapter 19:
Aquil Bassett

Aquil Bassett
President, Jami Sales

Influence
the Influencers.

In the 1990s, Abdullah Abdur-Rabbani and Aquil Bassett both provided jobs for my friends and me with their t-shirt printing businesses. I was team Rabbani, so we witnessed Aquil's business genius primarily as rivals.

Anytime Aquil took a team to an event that we were working, we'd get a peek at their shirts and laugh. "Man, Quil and them's shirts are wack this time. Our design is crushing theirs!" Every time, we'd say this, and it was probably true. Abdullah had us influencing and designing his shirts, while Aquil's crew was typically older. So our designs were going to be fresher, in every sense of the word.

But when it was time to work that beach, strip, or stadium, Aquil would show up with a team of 15-20 salesmen and 500 dozen color shirts. We would be about 5-7 deep with about 200 dozen white shirts. Quil's team would flood the area with shirts all day Friday and Saturday morning. They would start working discounts way before we were ready to, but force our hand. So even though we would sell out, their "inferior" shirts would win the weekend by sheer volume and strategy.

Aquil was teaching a master class on supply, demand, and market manipulation to anyone paying attention. And plenty of us were paying attention.

Aquil took the same approach to real estate, apparel licensing, and several other opportunities over the years. One real estate investment that he made as a 19-year-old was vital to the growth of Imam Jamil Al-Amin's community. He still owns the deed.

In an era where Atlanta Influences Everything and everyone has a clothing line or a t-shirt shop, understand that Aquil Bassett is the one that influenced Atlanta. From Aquil's Jami Sales and Abdullah's Thirsty Camel Sales came R. World Shirt Company, and from R. World came popular brands like Kosher, Hustler By Nature, Faith Family Funds, Creative Ink, Ready to Go Printing, and many more.

Aquil Bassett has quietly shaped the culture of success in Atlanta for four decades, and his influence is still growing.

Aquil Bassett is a Giant in Our Midst.

GIANT PRINCIPLE:

Influence the Influencers.
Don't follow every wave,
be the wave.

Chapter 20:
Demetricus Holloway

Demetricus Holloway
Server/Farmer

"Everything good in life
is in the middle."

looked up from the chessboard to see if I could detect a hint of an uncle joke. Because, the way my pubescent brain was set up, that sounded a little risqué coming from my Aunt Kim's husband. But he kept his gaze on the board as he moved his knight from g8 to f6. "You want to control the center of the board. If you control the center, you control the game."

Demetricus 'Idris' Holloway was talking about rows c through f on the board, but this may well have been his life's motto.

Fresh out of FAMU, Demetricus and his new wife, my mother's younger sister, was back in his hometown of Atlanta and broke. But you would never know it based on how happy and well-adjusted they always seemed. My ever-cheerful aunt worked at Goran's Ice Cream shop at the Underground. I have no idea what Demetricus did besides teaching me his philosophies on centeredness and attention to detail through chess and basketball.

"Defense starts with balance, nephew. Spread your feet shoulder-width apart."

"On your toes! Be proactive, not reactive."

"Don't look at the ball, or my eyes or my feet, I can juke you with those. Look at the center.

Never take your eyes off the waist…"

One day, Demetricus got a call from his college buddy Will Packer asking if he could help on the set of a film called Trois. Demetricus said sure and earned an assistant costume designer credit, despite never having sewn a stitch his entire life.

By the time I visited Los Angeles in 2005 to tour a film school, Demetricus was a self-taught master tailor who had established himself as one of Hollywood's go-to set customers.

A set costumer is the person in charge of the most central aspect of a film's authenticity — the clothes that characters wear. Movies are not shot linearly. The last scene could be shot first and the first scene last. The costumer has to be organized and meticulous enough to have every detail in place no matter when the scenes are shot. And they have to ensure the actors behave properly in their clothes between takes.

Demetricus' philosophies were being tested on the world's biggest stage, and he was controlling the game.

With hits like Drumline, The Fighting Temptations, Coach Carter, and the Longest Yard under his belt, his star was rising, but he was doing it behind the scenes.

I could relate to that.

When I returned to LA again in 2019 as a film producer, I set up a breakfast meeting with the grizzled Hollywood vet. He walked in in full distinguished gentleman mode, with his frost-tipped beard, crisp white button-up, blazer, pressed blue jeans, and a briefcase that matched his shiny brown shoes. He informed us that he was wrapping up 'The Little Things' with Denzel and spoke of him and other top stars like you or I would address any of our co-workers. He expressed confidence that he could get us in front of some heavy hitters.

After the meeting with my team, I leveled with him in private; I needed his help navigating the industry, access to some of his relationships, and wanted to see 'Producer' next to his name on IMDB.

He said in his deliberate way, "You've got the story, and you've got the plan. You're controlling the center of the board. I'm in."

My man…
Demetricus Holloway is Black History in the Making.
He is a Giant in Our Midst.

GIANT PRINCIPLE:

*Stay Balanced, and you'll
control the board.*

Chapter 21:
Omar Regan

Omar Regan
is no joke.

Sure, he is hilarious and has a grin that can light up any room he steps in. And yes, he probably does a better James Carter impersonation than Chris Tucker himself at this point. But the man's accomplishments are no laughing matter. When you get to know him, it quickly becomes clear why.

I met Omar like most people do these days — as an audience member. Granted, he was a teenager making fun of his father's infamous friends at a Riyaadah – basically the Black Muslim Olympics. But, like today, Omar was the star in the room that day. His way of making everyone he interacted with feel like the most important person to him at that moment made his success as an entertainer feel inevitable.

Sure enough, nowadays, when Omar is not breaking barriers as a movie writer/director/producer/star, he's speaking the universal language of laughter to audiences worldwide.

But the tragic murder of his father in 2009 forced Omar to start showing another side of himself.

The son of Detroit's famed Imam Luqman Abdullah, Omar was often considered the preacher's wholesome kid but kind of a class clown. But when his father passed, it activated a new level of Omar's intellect. Omar began to take on an activist role, fighting to clear misconceptions about his father's death. He even began to step into his father's shoes as a powerful speaker and teacher when called upon.

In conversations about screenwriting, dialogue, and acting, he reveals a relentless drive to learn everything about his craft. Sure, it pulls back the curtain on the myth that Omar Regan is where he is due to sheer God-given talent and that he's just up there being himself. But it gives way to a much more impressive reality: That beneath the funny, Omar Regan is a hard-working, calculated, genius-level talent who is only getting better.

So yes, laugh at Omar in 'American Sharia' when you rent it on Amazon Prime. Laugh at his impersonations when he comes to your city to close out that banquet.

Just as long as you remember, Omar Regan, the man, is no joke.

Omar Regan is a Giant in Our Midst.

GIANT PRINCIPLE:

Have a sense of humor, but you must be dead serious about honing your craft.

Chapter 22:
Amir Sulaiman

Amir Sulaiman is
the greatest poet
on earth.

I don't say this from the perspective of a poetry guru.

I have not searched the globe for men and women who spit with the perfect blend of profundity, cadence, and rhyme. I just know what I feel when hearing something undeniably dope. I know how difficult it is to create art that gets increasingly more profound with each listen. More complex with each read. And every poem I have ever heard Amir spit has these qualities.

Atlanta in the 2000s was home to many of the best spoken word artists, and often still, I rolled my eyes at predictable punchlines and rhyme schemes while others snapped and nodded.

But Amir is different.

It's not every day that a former English teacher and Harvard fellow who looks like he can play linebacker for your favorite NFL team walks on a stage and takes even a poetry skeptic such as myself through a gamut of emotions.

Awe, at the dexterity of his wordplay.

Reverence, because of the power and passion in his voice.

Empathy for the voiceless whose behalf he speaks on.

Anger at the monsters at whom he has aimed.

Love, because he demands it again and again.

All in a few short minutes.

"I'm a teenage Palestinian
Opening fire at an Israeli checkpoint, point-blank,
check-mate, now what?!
I'm a rape victim with a gun cocked to his cock, cock BANG!
Bangkok! Now what?!
I am Sitting Bull with Colonel Custer's scalp in my hands
I am Cinque with a slave trader's blood on my hands
I am Jonathan Jackson handing a gun to my man
I am David with a slingshot and a rock
And if David lived today, he'd have a Molotov cocktail and a Glock."

If you have ever sat in a room when Amir reaches this part of his poem "Danger" and didn't get goosebumps, you are not among the free and living. If you have not, seek it.

Amir Sulaiman is the greatest poet on earth.

Not because he was featured on Russell Simmons' Def Poetry Jam on HBO.

Not because he is Grammy-nominated or because the shows he has written and produced have garnered Emmy, Golden Globe, and Peabody nominations.

Not because he has performed across the US as well as England, Belgium, Senegal, Saudi Arabia, Sweden, Australia, Iran, and the Netherlands, and continues to tour worldwide.

It's because he is an English teacher disproving the "those who cannot do…" myth.

It's because he's a large Black man that had to learn to use words to put people at ease.

It's because he's hip-hop.

It's because he went to Persia to immerse himself in the art form he has humbly sought to master.

It's because he went live at 11:11 PM on IG every night for a month to allow us into his process and gain insight from his listeners.

Simply put, the man is a master of his craft.

Amir Sulaiman is Black History in the Making.
He is a Giant in Our Midst.

GIANT PRINCIPLE:

Learn to use words
as your weapons.

Chapter 23:
Khalil Ismail

Khalil Ismail
Community Advocate | Emcee

It's easiest to see greatness
in those with strengths that
are opposite your own.

When you come from a community that has been dealt decades' worth of bad hands, there is no wrong way to make positive change.

Whether we write, speak, perform, donate, build, or inspire, the more we do to improve the condition of our people, the more likely we are to encounter others on the same mission. But it's also more likely that we find people with different approaches to the mission.

For instance, I care about improving the condition of humanity, but it's not always obvious to those that don't know me. I'm an introvert and more analytical than empathetic. So if I'm not careful, I skip over the heart work and jump to problem-solving.

On the other hand, if "I just want to better understand" was a person, it would be Khalil Ismail. Deeply sensing and empathetic, Khalil wears his heart on his sleeve and has a way of convincing others to dig deep and bear all with him. He gets to the heart of the matter.

I've known of Khalil for many years. I've had his music on my playlists, met his family members, coached against his basketball team, and seen him at plenty of events. He's a staple in the community. So a formal introduction wasn't necessary when I ran into him in a huddle with some of my closest friends at a conference two years ago.

I was fresh off a disappointing encounter with some of the gatekeepers of our community and a little heated. Khalil assumed the role of therapist and helped turn it into a productive discourse between a who's who of young Muslim leaders from around the country about our responsibility as the next torchbearers to gently but firmly assume control without asking permission.

Just another day's work for one of this Renaissance's most versatile talents.

You need a journalist? A Master of Ceremonies? 16 bars that will make you nod your head and think? Someone to organize and promote your event better than it's ever been done? Call Khalil.

Khalil Ismail calls himself a Creative Director, Emcee, Vocalist, Community Advocate, Thinker, and Speaker.
I call **Khalil Ismail** a Giant in Our Midst.

GIANT PRINCIPLE:

Be versatile.

Chapter 24:
Imani Bilal

Art is powerful.

Throughout history, the mood of a time is best captured by artists. Historians have all the facts of an era. Philosophers have all the pressing questions. But artists are the ones tasked with communicating the experience of an age. The mood. The sentiment.

Historical acts are subject to the perspectives of the writer and reader. Time often exposes the philosopher's conclusion as laughable. But there is no medium between art and its consumer. Not opinion, not education, not time, not distance. Art is a direct expression from one soul to another.

When Sam Cooke's 'A Change is Gonna Come' plays in Spike Lee's 'Malcolm X,' I'm in the car with Malcolm, summoning up courage as he drives to certain death.

When Jean-Michel Basquiat continuously goes back to the skull as a starting place to express himself, often depicting an explosion of some sort coming from the head, I feel the torture of having so many things to say with so little time. Or the perfectly articulated musings of an overstimulated, active mind.

I began to collect Imani Bilal's work last year because it reminded me of an upgrade on classic abstract expressionist painters such as Morris Louis or Jackson Pollock. Both of them are considered geniuses of the genre, but for me, they were either too simplistic (Louis) or too dense (Pollock.)

Imani incorporates dichotomy in each of her paintings. Dark, bright. Layered, monochromatic. Fire, water. Simple, dense. All in the same work. Then she tops it off with Quranic themes or verses.

When Jihan received a pair of Imani's earrings as a gift, and then I saw her art would be displayed in a Manhattan gallery in an exhibit called Fingerprints of Ruh (Soul), I sensed the best-kept secret portion of Imani's career was coming to an end. It kinda feels like when your favorite song on an album becomes a single on the radio, and now everyone is singing it. My senses proved to be correct when Imani was featured in Forbes magazine not long after the series concluded. Now we know for certain we have someone dope from our tribe repping this era's experience, mood, and sentiment in the annals of art history.

I guess I'll just be the first to say…
Imani Bilal is Black History in the Making.
She is a Giant in Our Midst.

GIANT PRINCIPLE:

Create a beautiful legacy.

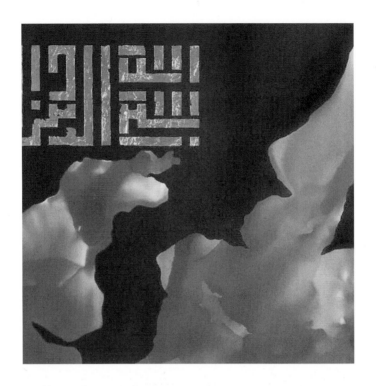

Chapter 25:
Kairi Al-Amin

Kairi Al-Amin
CEO, West End Music Group

Expectations
are like parachutes.

Depending on your direction, they can hold you up or back.

When they're holding you up, it's a matter of delaying an inevitable fall. You will either quit or get stronger when they're holding you back.

Kairi Al-Amin has grappled with the gifts and curses of expectation his entire life. The son of Civil Rights icon and political prisoner Jamil Al-Amin (formerly known as H. Rap Brown), and respected attorney Karima Al-Amin, the expectations for Kairi were sky-high from an early age. People would observe him, notice his exceptional talents and wonder out loud if he would be a world-renowned speaker. Professional athlete? Lawyer? Imam?

Mediocrity was never an option.

The expectations grew as Kairi continued to excel academically, ultimately becoming an attorney himself. People expected him to be a civil rights attorney that dedicated his career to getting his father's conviction overturned. But he chose contract law, and used it to get into the music industry managing artists. They expected him to eventually take over his mother's firm. He opened a hookah lounge. They expected him to make it Muslim-friendly. He made it one of the most successful after-hours spots in downtown Atlanta.

Kairi bucked the system that raised him and was shunned for it. People thought he was crazy. Disrespectful. His response? He became a rapper.

Kairi was tired of being held up by the expectations thrust on the son of great parents. He made decision after decision that put the parachute at his back but made him much stronger.

With that strength, Kairi's advocacy on behalf of his father in the past two years has surpassed all 18 years worth of previous efforts combined. He understands that it is a battle best fought in the court of public opinion, not the court of law. His label, West End Music Group, is putting up streaming numbers that major labels are spending hundreds of thousands to reach. And the music actually bangs.

And he's just getting started. You'll see.
Kairi Al-Amin is a Giant in Our Midst.

GIANT PRINCIPLE:

Choose Your Adventure.
Don't let anyone else
write your story.

Chapter 26:
Dr. Marcus Lambert

The Model Akh

One day, Jihan overheard some of my friends and I refer to my friend Jamil as the model Akh (short for Akhi, which means brother in Arabic). Jamil is a great brother, and everything we said about him reflected that, but the word 'Jamil' never came out of our mouths.

Afterward, she asked, "who is this Model Brother that you guys were talking about?" I realized by her intonation that she thought we were saying this brother was so exemplary to us that we used him as a standard, a model of how Akhs should be.

I cracked up. "No, Jamil is literally a model. Like, photoshoots and runways." She joined me in laughter, but what followed was a thought exercise about who would, in fact, be the Model Akh.

We decided that the Model Akh would be spiritual, educated, married, a good father, active in the community, cultured, adventurous, humble, handsome, fit, an earner, and funny. From that point on, whenever we would encounter a brother who met some of the criteria, we would weigh his candidacy as The Model Akh.

In the summer of 2015, we took a family trip to New York City during Ramadan. We spent days showing the kids Times Square, Coney Island, the MOMA, Central Park, and the World Trade Center while fasting from 5:15 AM to 8:30 PM. So the City that Never Sleeps would have to live up to its nickname for it not to be a trip from Hell. It didn't disappoint.

One of the planned evenings involved meeting for iftar (dinner) with a couple that we didn't know except from online exchanges.

The wife, Zahara, picked a nice halal restaurant, and the conversation between myself and the husband, Marcus, spanned from leadership strategies for our senior communities to parenting twins, their charity works around the city, and finally, some of his interests in the advances in experimental medicine and biology.

The next night, Marcus and I went to an iftar in Brooklyn. We arrived at the flat, and it was packed wall to wall with young Muslim professionals from varying backgrounds. The food was plentiful, and conversations flowed freely. I worked my way around the room and met some inspiring people making moves in the financial sector. I noticed Marcus doing the same. But after a while, we realized that there was a 'single Muslims meet' component to the event that wasn't for us, so we made our way out after Maghrib.

We decided to walk eight blocks to the nearest Masjid to make Isha and tawarih prayers. Halfway through the first block, the sky opened up, and, in an instant, rain drenched us. Marcus gave me a funny look like, "I'll run for it if you can hang."

So I took off.

Now I'm in a semi-competition to keep pace with this lanky, soft-spoken, unassuming dude that I just met, and he's moving steadily. I'm thinking, there's no way this dude will outrun me. We're splashing puddles, wiping rainwater pouring into our eyes, and navigating Brooklyn traffic for seven blocks until he slows up and smoothly walks inside a small Masjid as if nothing happened. We had to wring out our socks before we lined up to pray.

When I returned to the hotel that night, my wife asked me how it went.

I said, "So, I had to Google this Brother to find out he was a doctor. He married well, is a lowkey leader in the community, takes spontaneous trips around the world with his wife and kids, makes extra prayers, can run eight blocks in the rain without breathing hard, knows how to work a room, AND looks like a young Laurence Fishburne if he played Malcolm X? Yeah… I'm pretty sure I've found The Model Akh."

Dr. Marcus Lambert is Black History in the Making.
He is a Giant in Our Midst.

GIANT PRINCIPLE:

Be a model of integrity,
support, and focus.

Chapter 27:
Musa Siddeeq

Musa Siddeeq
Solutions Architect

"Do not present a problem to Musa
unless you want him to engage you
for more data with the goal
of finding a solution."

Nervous, I thumbed through the pages of my small legal pad for the umpteenth time. I was scanning my prepared remarks for a panel discussion that Noor Jihan and I were on, and it was almost time to go on stage.

"What's that?"

I looked up and saw Musa Siddeeq, the tech guy I was working with to build a website for my copywriting business. He and his wife, Summiyah, were on the same panel.

"Oh, just going over my notes," I replied.

Musa scoffed. "Notes? For this? Just wing it!"

I laughed with him but asked: "You don't have any notes?"

He said, "Psshh! No, man, come on… we've been preparing for this our whole life!"

He got up and walked confidently on stage with Sumiyyah. Then he looked back and called over his shoulder, "Leave that notebook!"

I didn't listen. I hid the notebook under my arm and took it onstage with me. But I tucked it under the table and decided I would only use it in case of an emergency.

In the next hour, Summiyah, Musa, Noor Jihan, and I stole the show with witty, authentic, and insightful dialogue that left the audience wanting more. By the end, Musa and I were having a lowkey punchline contest. It was by far my best public speaking performance to that date.

I walked off the stage with "I've been preparing for this my whole life" ringing so loudly in my head that I almost forgot my notebook.

I haven't used notes on a panel since.

Musa is a senior solutions architect and software developer for Turner that stays in character. Do not present a problem to Musa unless you want him to engage you for more data with the goal of finding a solution.

In 2019, Musa & Summiyah, Marcus & Zahara, Ayyub & Ndola, and a few other friends and family joined Noor Jihan and me at a resort in Cancun to celebrate our 10th anniversary. Each day we rode boats, explored caves, toured ruins, and dove into cenotes, but the dinners were the most memorable.

We'd laugh, joke, and compare notes on issues plaguing our communities. Musa would then facilitate a think tank session, making us devise solutions we could implement when we got home.

Summiyah and Musa married in their teens and have been together for more than half their lives, recently celebrating their 20th anniversary. They enjoy the benefits of starting a family early, with their children starting to go off to college and freeing them up for more ventures and leisure. Summiyah is co-founder of Nura and Sol, a sustainable swim/resort-wear brand designed for every coverage level. Musa teaches coding at his alma mater, Georgia Tech, has taken up cycling as a hobby, and has biked roads and trails all over the world. They recently bought the neighborhood halal meat store in order to continue a tradition of convenience for Muslims looking for ethically sourced meat. I love to see them enjoying their success.

They've been preparing for it their entire lives.

Musa Siddeeq is Black History in the Making.
He is a Giant in Our Midst.

GIANT PRINCIPLE:

Exude confidence and trust that you belong in every room you set foot in. You've been preparing all your life!

Chapter 28:
Dr. Flojaune Griffin-Cofer

Dr. Flojaune G. Cofer
Epidemiologist

We often associate humility with
meekness, shyness, or timidity.

On the other hand, we view assertiveness as a degree on the vanity spectrum.

But mix humility with assertiveness, discernment, and purpose, and you get genuine confidence. Sprinkle in a bleeding heart for the less fortunate and an obsession with Batman, and you get Flojaune 'Flo" Griffin-Cofer.

One of California's foremost epidemiologists and Public Health Advocates, Flo has never been called shy or timid.

If Flo is in a room, you know it before entering it. If someone is standing on the couch debating with her outside voice when you open the door, it's Flo.

Yet, she is one of the most humble people you will ever meet and the furthest from vain.

In the Summer of 2019, my son qualified for the Junior Olympics as a sprinter. Flo insisted to my wife, her fellow Spelmanite, and line sister that my son and I stay at her place, only a couple miles from the venue.

Flo monitored my son's race times online and was sure to be there screaming her head off when it was his heat before unmuting whoever was in her earpiece and retreating to work.

But the nights at Flo's house felt like something out of a sitcom.

It felt like a nonstop party between Flo's house guests, pets, neighbors who walked in unannounced, and co-workers who had food labeled in her fridge. They treated each other as siblings, and the debates were never-ending.

At first, it seemed like fun and games until I realized we were think-tanking some of Sacramento's most pressing problems, and Flo happened to be a person that could turn the solutions into policy the following day.

Flo's infatuation with Batman comes from her belief that, like Batman, she has no superpower but is committed to her community and stops forces that hurt her neighbors.

But she can't be Batman because she doesn't care enough about money. And she does have a superpower — her humility. So praise is her Kryptonite.

Compliment or tell her the obvious, that she is supposed to be the mayor of Sacramento, for instance, and she gets downright meek.

It's the weirdest thing.

Dr. Flojaune Cofer is Black History in the Making.
She is one of the Giants in My Midst.

GIANT PRINCIPLE:

Fight the powers that be – and remember:
Humble Does Not mean Meek!

Chapter 29:
Cornell Wesley

Cornell Wesley
Economic Developer

"One cannot have a global impact
with a domestic mindset. We simply
must create an ecosystem that
concerns itself with the urban core."

I once participated in a panel discussion about code-switching. Last to answer out of eight panelists, I was the only one to have a positive spin on the subject. I said it's not much different from being bilingual and that those who can pull it off should be compensated for their translation ability. I got a ton of side-eyes.

A few weeks later, I was in the audience as a stately, classically suited, and well-spoken brother went before a group of white bankers and CEOs and told them in the conclusion of his speech, "One cannot have a global impact with a domestic mindset. We simply must create an ecosystem that concerns itself with the urban core."

He got a rousing ovation as he graciously shook hands with the scrum of execs looking to connect with him. When he got to me, I held my hand out for a firm shake, but before I could say "great speech," he dapped me up, pulled me in, and said in a low tone, "These muf*ckas don't know what just hit em. I gotta get to the next presentation, but make sure you holla at me before you dip." Then he walked off.

I had to look at my program again.

It wasn't hard to spot a cheesing 'Cornell Wesley, United States EDA' among the sea of white faces. Not only did this man clearly subscribe to my code-switching theory, but he was the one who decided where millions of federal dollars went, and he had just told the CEOs that wanted those dollars, "If you don't rock with the hood, I'm not rocking with you," but in the King's English.

You can be certain I made sure to holla at him before I left.

These days when I call him about a project, we skip pleasantries and get straight to it. His response is either no or "it's on" within two minutes. Sometimes he's cutting me off with "say less" before I even get the pitch out. After a while, he was just the homie Cornell.

One day, I came across an article saying that the last sitting governor, a middle-aged white Republican woman, had signed with EMBLEM Strategies — the firm Cornell formed after leaving the EDA. "Of course she did," I chuckled.

Today, Cornell is one of the most powerful men in his hometown of Birmingham, Alabama, after accepting the Chief Economic Development Officer role when his Morehouse brother and mayor Randall L. Woodfin offered it to him.

Cornell Wesley is Black History in the Making.
He is a Giant in Our Midst.

GIANT PRINCIPLE:

Use the language necessary to be heard and get the job done. Codeswitching is bankable talent. Just don't forget to add it to the invoice.

Chapter 30:
Maurianna Adams

In July 2018, I was hired to facilitate a
board retreat for a nonprofit group.

On arriving at the location of the retreat, I recognized T. Sheri Dickerson - President of the Oklahoma BLM chapter, Jacobi Ryan - a financial advisor Fresh off a strong showing on a panel with Angela Rye, Chelsey Branham - a soon-to-be State Representative, Dr. Noel Jacobs - Psychologist and President of the Interfaith Alliance and Veronica Laizure - Civil Rights Attorney for the Council of American Islamic Relations Oklahoma.

Impressive group.

So naturally, I began to look around for the leader, Maurianna Adams, whom I spoke with on the phone in preparation. Anyone that this group has selected to lead them had to be... what's better than impressive? Spectacular?

Well, after the meeting, I wrote in my consult report:

"At several junctions in our discussion, the group alluded to what I consider to be its most pressing issue: Accountability. Or more specifically, a lack thereof. President Maurianna Adams has conditioned the other members of the group to expect her to either complete or clean up every task put before the group. By acting as a safety net for everyone, Mrs. Adams has handicapped the group. As such, the group has not grown to be equal to the sum of its parts..."

Ouch, right?

Well, they didn't pay me to make them feel good.

But think about it, if your biggest weakness is shining too bright, you're in great shape. This group of accomplished and influential leaders saw so much integrity, work ethic, and potential in a young Maurianna that they were often content to watch her work her magic, like a rookie year Kobe.

Maurianna's moves in just 18 months since show that she has learned how to pass responsibility to others.

In an Oklahoma City political scene rife with opportunities for new leaders to emerge, Maurianna has done so as a super-connector. In her role as Executive Director for Progress OKC, she forms public-private partnerships and broad cross-sector coordination across the city. In her advocacy on behalf of political candidates for city or state seats, her presence signals to voters who the integrity candidate is.

Her growing political cache caught the eye of OKC Mayor David Holt when he appointed Maurianna, Councilwoman Nikki Nice, and Dr. Quentin Hughes to co-chair the new task force for human rights, where she has helped to build a network that doubles as a who's who of OKC activism.

The only thing left for Maurianna to do is pick which office she wants to take. Because the city knows that if she ever decides to, she is now ready to win as the alpha.

Maurianna Adams is Black History in the Making.
She is a Giant in Our Midst.

GIANT PRINCIPLE:

Don't do the most just because you can;
it's not sustainable. Learn to delegate.

Chapter 31:
Charity Marcus

They have Black people
in Oklahoma?

get this question a lot. In most people's minds, Oklahoma is just one of the 30 or so states in between the good stuff. I'm coming up on a decade here, and people I grew up with still ask, "Where are you again? Kansas? Colorado? Wyoming?"

I get it.

When people talk about Black History in America, they like to put it in a nice Southeastern frame, with a little ChiTown for good measure. When they reference Black Wall Street, in their minds, it's basically just Wakanda in black and white.

But energy cannot be created nor destroyed, only transferred. When blood spills, the soil preserves its essence. And the energy of a great movement reverberates for decades.

Charity Marcus is a daughter of Tulsa. A strategic consultant and public relations expert, she has risen from its soil every bit the modern embodiment of the folks who built, then rebuilt Black Wall Street a century ago.

When Charity showed up at one of Maurianna Adams' networking events in 2019, I kept my eye on the door, half expecting a team of Gladiators to file in behind her. I didn't know who she was but gathered that I probably should. I learned that Charity runs political campaigns for conservative candidates during election years, so the Olivia Pope vibe made perfect sense. But it made me wonder how many self-taught, unapologetically Black women in the world could say that they told older Republican men what to do for a living.

When I was added to the production team for a period film set in Tulsa, I called Charity for a lay of the land. She casually pulled in State Rep. Regina Goodwin, granddaughter of the owners of the Black newspaper that was burned down during the massacre. Over lunch, they conveyed to me that Tulsa is a resilient community that still has open wounds from the events that took place on May 31, 1921.

But they are far from victims.

On top of running her PR firm and her political consultancy, Charity is co-founder of Black Women Business Owners of America. In 2019, Charity was named to the Governor's Minority Business Council. In 2020, she appeared with Maurianna on Governor Kevin Stitt's Roundtable on Race.

So yes, Oklahoma has Black people. And the richest Black History in America. Thanks to movers like Charity, its future is in very capable hands.

Charity Marcus is Black History in the Making.
She is a Giant in Our Midst.

GIANT PRINCIPLE:

Honor your ancestors by speaking truth to power.

Chapter 32:
Shareef Abdul-Malik

Shareef Abdul-Malik
CEO, WeBuyBlack

Well before he turned
30 years old,
Shareef Abdul-Malik
was a man's man.

Humble, creative, able to protect himself with or without weapons, and successful — Shareef is the kind of man you want your son to become and your daughter to marry.

But this story is not a coming-of-age story.

Don't get me wrong; I'd love to write a charming tale about the hard knocks that shaped a boy into the man who created the world's largest Black-Owned business platform. But Shareef has behaved like a grown man most of his life.

Before he graduated college and launched WeBuyBlack.com, Shareef was one of those kids that carried himself with the swag of an older man. Confident in speech and consistent in action, we stopped treating him like we did his peers after a while. He was just Shareef, the young man who would succeed regardless.

Shareef got married while still at W.D. Mohammed high school. Eh, sounds about right.

Shareef is the MSA President at Howard University, giving speeches on the D.C. streets? He'd better be.

Shareef is on track to becoming the Black Jeff Bezos? Naturally.

In April 2018, I helped spearhead a conference and needed a dynamic young keynote speaker who could speak to the event's theme - Illuminating the Faith: Calculated Steps Toward Prosperity. I shut down all suggestions and called Shareef.

When I picked Shareef up from the airport, he first asked about how far Black Wall Street was and whether we may have time to visit it. "Fitting that the man who created the closest thing to Black Wall Street that we have today would ask that," I said.

It was then that I began to understand that Shareef, with all of his self-awareness and success, had no idea how big of a deal he is. He told me how honored I was that I invited him because this was his first paid speaking engagement and keynote.

Through my shock, I told him, "Well, you're a paid keynote speaker now. Go get some more. The world needs to know Shareef Abdul-Malik exists."

Shareef Abdul-Malik is Black History in the Making.
He is a Giant in Our Midst.
P.S. He killed the speech. But you already figured that.

GIANT PRINCIPLE:

Be mindful that youth is fleeting.
Take advantage of it to build
generational wealth.

Chapter 33:
Faruq Hunter

Sometimes I wonder what
certain historical figures would
be like in the modern age.

Would George Washington Carver be a capitalist? Would Booker T. Washington be a Republican or Democrat? Would George Washington Williams be a patriot? Would any of those three change their names? Would Umar ibn Al-Khattab be viewed more as a political genius, theologian, or military mastermind?

In Faruq Hunter, I feel like I'm getting an answer to some of these questions. Whenever Faruq and I see each other, we have a ritual. He comes over, shouts to the room about how debonair I am, and I say something about how we are all in the presence of one of the smartest, most ingenuitive men of our time. The embrace that follows confirms that we are both sincere.

Faruq is a real throwback. He is ambitious, resourceful, and unapologetic. He cuts an imposing physical figure, but he is more interested in discussing the latest technological advances than hurting anyone. You get the sense that you could drop him anywhere between the Stone Age and the Civil Rights era, and he would be great.

Faruq's Freedom Nation is what happens when you drop a great man, cut from the cloth of eras past, into a hyper-capitalist society wherein doing for self is a lost art.

Founded on the principle that Black people are too dependent on the government and corporations for their survival, Freedom Nation began as a small town in Georgia. The entire village produces its electricity, water, and natural gas on an internally developed distributed energy production Smart Grid. No resource on the 200+ acre lot is wasted; trees are repurposed as lumber, and the Georgia red clay is compressed into bricks. Freedom Nation also has a currency system based on merit and sweat equity.

Today, Faruq can be found expanding Freedom Nation, literally in South Central Siberia. As I said, drop him anywhere, and he'll thrive.

When the apocalypse comes, I know where I'll be. I'll be busy trying to be the debonair Ambassador for one of our time's smartest, most ingenuitive men.

The Georgia location, though.

Farouq Hunter is Black History in the Making.
He is a Giant in Our Midst.

GIANT PRINCIPLE:

The earth is spacious. Don't limit yourself to where you start your life as you seek to build your empire. Make hijrah if necessary.

Chapter 34:
Bryan "Ibrafall" Wright

Bryan Ibrafall Wright
Urban Agriculturalist

Getting back to our roots
can manifest itself
in many ways.

Black history is not only a story of resourcefulness and resilience. It is also a love story between man and creation. Of wealth and abundance. It is utilizing every resource that God has given us to be of benefit to those whose lives we touch and showing gratitude for the earth's resources by leaving it better than we found it.

Bryan 'Ibrafall' Wright embodies all these ideals with his work as an urban agriculturalist. His love and knowledge of soil, plants, and climate come out of his pores.

But his love for his own people is much deeper.

For Ibrafall, a fully funded 20-acre farm in the middle of nowhere is not appealing. Neither is the fancy tenured professorship gig at a top University. He is offered these kinds of opportunities all the time. For an opportunity to make sense to Ibrafall, it has to keep his hands in the soil and directly benefit his people.

The Northeast side of Oklahoma City is the historically Black side of town and a notorious food desert. Through his Black Urban Gardening Society (BUGS) group, Ibrafall noticed that most urban centers share this issue. But aside from the fast-food restaurants and liquor stores that tend to be on every block in the hood, Ibrafall noted that there are also churches.

So he developed a plan to combat food deserts by setting up gardens at those churches and other houses of worship and farmer's markets for them to sell and/or distribute the crops.

I did everything in my power to make our Masjid one of the first communities to take Ibrafall up on his proposal. With Ibrafall at the helm, a group of Brothers and Sisters from the community carried Ibrafall's vision to perfection and reaped substantial summer and fall harvests in 2020 and 2021.

With more people at home and conscious of the reality that normalcy can be snatched at any time, BUGS is blowing up with over 10,000 members and climbing and a new viral Facebook commercial. People want to return to their roots, and Ibrafall will be there with a shovel, showing them how.

He's as down-to-earth as they come, but
Ibrafall Wright is Black History in the Making.
He's a Giant in Our Midst.

GIANT PRINCIPLE:

Cultivate and care for the planet;
it will take care of you.

Chapter 35:
Basheerah Ahmad

Sometimes past success can be a
shadow that is hard to shake.

Our society is so conditioned to label people and keep them in their boxes that we will downright refuse to recognize their growth.

Basheerah Ahmad comes from a long line of incredible women, including her sisters. Aquilah is a brilliant engineer and women's health advocate who builds websites in her spare time. Iman is a gifted actress, teacher, and business manager. You've met Noor Jihan.

Their mother, Joy, is a Stanford-educated educator and her mother was a mathematician when that sort of thing was unheard of for Black women. The women in their extended family consist of Doctors, Emmy-winning producers, School directors, and the list goes on.

Growing up, Basheerah was an accomplished dancer and beauty queen. Her gregarious attitude, poise, and polished speaking ability led to her winning several pageants, including Miss Black America.

She did not peak there.

True to her family's educational tradition, she obtained a Bachelors's and two Master's degrees and is now best known as a Celebrity Fitness Expert featured on Dr. Phil, The Doctors, The Today Show, and plenty more.

But there is more to Basheerah than what meets the eye.

People readily give Basheerah credit for her fitness, looks, dancing, or anything else physical, completely dismissing the hard work and determination she has poured into her education and career. The unspoken insinuation is that because of her looks, she was bound to be successful.

In 2013, Basheerah went to Tanzania to scale Mount Kilimanjaro with a large group of professional athletes and climbers.

She was one of only a handful to reach the peak.

Since that day, Basheerah's love of the continent of Africa deepened. She formed an International Business consulting firm, Mothers

Reserve, that has brokered deals between US firms and the government of Botswana. She then returned stateside and launched a fitness clothing line called Born Warrior that caters to people often overlooked by sportswear companies.

Despite her success, Basheerah stays grounded by tending to animals on the family land back home. Basheerah and I have braved -1 degree weather to feed cows and goats during an ice storm. Oklahoma is no Kilimanjaro, so if it were up to her, she would've done it alone. She's also the first person Jihan, and I call in a pinch to pick up the kids from school or a roadside rescue.

In 2021, after completing her Ph.D. in Natural Medicine, she officially became Basheerah Ahmad Ph.D., BBA, MHR, MS, CPT, CSNC. Or Dr. Basheerah for short. Not long after, she was named the Wellness Director for Steve Harvey Global.

It's time to give credit where credit is due. Basheerah Ahmad is a down-to-earth, talented, hard-working businesswoman who was once a beauty queen.

Not the other way around.

Basheerah Ahmad is Black History in the Making.
She is a Giant in Our Midst.

GIANT PRINCIPLE:

Beauty starts internally and is not guaranteed to last eternally. So invest in your spirit and mind.

Chapter 36:
Sabria Mills

It's rare that someone can
command a moment
without saying anything.

In her work as Secretary for a board on which we both sit, Sabria brings an orderly presence. Efficient and matter of fact, she wastes very little time and commands respect without ever having to demand it.

Sabria has built a brand centered around these same abilities in her professional life. On her Dope Muslim Woman podcast, Sabria is courteous but direct. When this directness takes her guests off guard, Sabria is content with allowing the uncomfortable silence to coax answers out.

Like any good journalist, Sabria prepares yet allows the guests' answers to guide the conversation. But the most effective tool that Sabria uses is that silence.

The Dope Muslim Woman podcast targets a demographic unaccustomed to getting positive media attention. Able to trace our beginnings just one or two generations back, Black American Muslims are arguably the youngest demographic on the planet. In the 1960s and 70s, the pioneers focused on the heavy lifting of building and maintaining brand-new communities. They accomplished this while dealing with the social ramifications of switching religions and names. All while fighting for fundamental human rights.

Islam's Reverence for the prophets Abraham and Muhammad, who both emphasized the need and prayed for children, led to a mandate within the growing Black Muslim communities to "populate this Deen (religion)." No matter what socioeconomic, mental health conditions, or trauma they were facing, Black American Muslims populated the Deen with sons and daughters and trusted that God would sort everything out. For many of the pioneers of Islam in America, there was no room for healing on the itinerary.

Many passed their trauma to the next generation.

When Sabria asks one of these daughters or sons about their spirit, mental health, or healing, there are often decades worth of suppression for them to overcome to answer. When they finally break that silence, the healing begins.

Well worth the uncomfortable wait.

Sabria Mills is a Giant in Our Midst.

GIANT PRINCIPLE:

Healing begins when you listen, have patience, and get comfortable with being uncomfortable.

Chapter 37:
Basheer Jones

Basheer Jones
Councilman, Poet

Black History In the Making

One Friday afternoon, I pulled up to the after-jummah food spot and saw a new face holding court with a mixture of some of the community's young akhs and old heads.

Before I even got to the crowd, I could see he was photoshoot fresh with a little bop, articulation, and charisma to his movements. Then I heard him refer to himself as the Truth.

This young Morehouse cat reminded me of... Me.

When I was young, I read Choose Your Own Adventure novels. In these books, the character would make it to a certain point, and you got to decide if he or she does one thing or another. Depending on your choice, you could either prosper or die. After a few more of these ciphers and encounters, it began to feel like Basheer Jones was me on a different adventure. One where I chose to live his truth out loud.

We were blessed with a similar toolkit but chose to use them much differently. Where I would dim my light or accept a background role in the name of humility, Basheer gladly took centerstage and relished the leadership responsibility. Where I was content with just my circle knowing I was a dope lyricist and writer, Basheer put everything that was in him out for the world to see.

In one song, Basheer rapped, "While they were making excuses, I was making it happen." And it dawned on me that's exactly what I was doing.

I was trying so hard to be humble that I had let it interfere with my ambition. It didn't dawn on me until then that some of the adults beating humility into my head were lowkey haters who didn't want me to surpass them.

Basheer was younger than me and still showed me that it was not just ok but necessary for people blessed with certain gifts to shine, as long as their hearts were in the right place.

Every Eid in Atlanta, Basheer liked to spit poems and raps in the park. Poet after poet would line up to soak up some of his shine as he played to the crowd with something for the real spitters, the poets, and the sisters. I'd usually just stand and listen for a little while, but Basheer always eyeballed me like, when is this guy gonna jump in? When I did decide to jump in, Basheer became the biggest hypeman — adlibbing, trying to predict the last word of each line, and wincing at the punch-lines like they physically cut him.

When one of the organizations I help lead brought Basheer to Oklahoma a couple of years back, he started with some of those poems from the park. After he was done, he launched into a passionate speech that had everyone at the edge of their seat with inspiration. Afterward, we kicked it for a while, and I showed him some of the business ventures I was working on. Somewhere in the conversation, he asked, "Do those Brothers back there know you can spit?"

"Nah," I replied with a laugh.

Basheer looked at me like he would never understand why anyone would keep talent to themselves. "Why not??"

'Why not could have been Basheer Jones' campaign slogan if not for 'One Cleveland.' Having ridden his passions, convictions, talent, and hard work to a Council seat in his hometown of Cleveland, Basheer set his eyes on the Mayor's seat next. He fell short of his goal, but those of us that know and love Basheer know that even mayorship would have only been a stepping stone for our Brother. Win or lose, this Brother will continue to live his Truth out loud, and the results will be historic.

Because **Basheer Jones** is Black History in the Making.
He is a Giant in Our Midst.

GIANT PRINCIPLE:

Live out loud!

Conclusion

How to Be a Giant

You are what you consume. So eat to live like Umi, don't live to eat. Instead, feed your mind and body with healthy, clean nourishment. Like sugar becomes fat fruits become energy, thoughts become speech, actions become habits, and habits become legacy.

Seek Truth, like Abu leaving Indianapolis for New York. **Peace is with those who follow their hearts.**

Be mindful that youth is fleeting. So take advantage of it to build generational wealth like Shareef Abdul-Malik.

Glow up NOW, like Farouq. You never know how much time you have to impact this earth.

Be Bold like Ebro. Keep your childlike creativity as long as you can. Then, build the best team and keep your aces in their places.

Take the Leap, like 6-year-old me, over the well. But not before knowing what you're getting yourself into.

Face Your Fears like Khalfani confronting bullies outside of Grady.

Stay Balanced like Demetricus Holloway, and you'll control the board.

Welcome the new, as Zak welcomed me to the Shed. A true star is confident that nothing can dim its light. There is room for everyone to shine.

Seek relevant knowledge and apply it daily, like Ariaka. Don't let your enrollment status interfere with your education.

Stand Tall like Imam Siraaj Wahhaj. Nothing can stand against you if the Creator is with you.

Stay Cool under fire like Imam Nadim Ali.

Be Humble like Imam Sulaimaan Hamed. Let your passion illuminate your community, and accept criticism with a twinkle in your eye.

Embody Wisdom, Serenity, and Greatness like Adeyinka Mendes. Make people wonder if you are connected to a higher power.

Have Faith (Iman) in your gifts and core beliefs, especially when life beats you down.

Shine Your Light on the world like Noor Jihan. Serve the underserved and light up every room with your smile.

Compete to do good like Ayyub Abdush-Shakur.

Influence the Influencers like Aquil Bassett. Be the wave.

Be dead serious about honing your craft like Omar Regan.

Learn to use words as your weapons, like Amir Sulaiman.

Be Versatile like Khalil Ismail.

Leave a legacy of creating beauty like Imani Bilal.

Choose Your Adventure like Kairi Al-Amin. Don't let anyone else write your story.

Like Dr. Marcus Lambert, **be a model of integrity, support, and focus.**

Fight the powers that be like Dr. Flojaune Griffin - and remember: **Humble Does Not mean Meek!**

Like Cornell Wesley, **use the language necessary to be heard** and get the job done. Codeswitching is bankable talent. Just don't forget to add it to the invoice.

Don't do the most just because you can; it's not sustainable. **Instead, learn to delegate** like Maurianna Adams.

Honor your ancestors and **speak truth to power** like Charity Marcus

Remember: The earth is spacious. Don't limit yourself to where you start your life as you seek to build your empire. Make hijrah if necessary, like Faruq Hunter.

Take cues from nature. **Cultivate and care for the planet** like Ibrafall Wright, and it will take care of you.

Beauty starts internally and is not guaranteed to last eternally. So **invest in your spirit and mind** like Basheerah Ahmad.

Know what you're for, not just what you're against. And **Always Be Closing** on it, like Brother Abdullah at a homecoming. Use what you've got to feed your family.

Never Quit, like Yaseen. Regardless of the hand you are dealt, everyone has royal potential. Plan and persevere. New frontiers await!

Take it from Sabria Mills; healing begins when you listen, have patience, and **get comfortable with being uncomfortable.**

Like April Dawn on a Greyhound, **stay aware of your surroundings** and **only invite positive energy into your space**. Adopt these qualities from the Giants in My Midst, and you will **be memorable**.

Live Out Loud like Basheer Jones.

And finally, **Exude confidence** and trust that you belong in every room you set foot in, like Musa Siddeeq. **You've been preparing all your life!**

BONUS: What I Learned About Overcoming Procrastination

Some people have a knack for taking care of business, while the rest of us have loose ends dangling all over our lives. If you struggle with completing essential tasks, you likely lack a strong work ethic.

There is no way around it. If you're fighting against The Nothing, understand it is a fight to the death! If you want to develop a powerful work ethic and get more done but feel like you're just unable to, no matter how hard you try, it doesn't mean you're lazy or destined to fail. It simply means you have to take proven steps to develop successful habits.

"If you think the price of success is high,
wait until you get the bill for regret."
~ Tim Grover

What exactly is a work ethic? It's a set of principles based on the idea that there is a moral virtue in hard work and persistence, where the joy is in the grind, not the destination.

You undoubtedly know people with solid work ethics and others lacking in this area. But, unsurprisingly, those with strong work ethics are also the ones who are always able to get more done.

Try these strategies to strengthen your work ethic:

1. **Learn to finish.** Many individuals have trouble getting started but seem to do well once that initial hurdle is cleared. Others are fine getting out of the gate but need help to complete anything. I'd get to the 90% complete point and find every excuse to delay that last 10%. It could be due to a fear of failure, or it could be due to a fear of success. Either way, done is better than perfect.

   - Many tasks are challenging to finish because the amount of time spent on the last 10% of the work can be considerable. Accomplishing some goals is like building a house - the final 5% of the job can take 20% of the time. It's all the little odds and ends that are time-consuming but fail to show visible progress.

   - Although it takes determination to see a project through to completion, once done, it's off your plate entirely. Finishing projects also frees up a lot of mental energy.

2. **Work longer.** Your body and mind get used to working for a certain amount of time. However, after that, your focus starts to wane, and mental exhaustion sets in.

   - If you take a break every time you feel like it, you'll fail to work any longer or harder than you do now.

   - Use a timer. See how long you can work before your performance starts to go downhill. Then, extend that period by 10% and keep working. Your ability to focus on your work for extended periods will increase. Be proud of the positive changes you see over time.

3. **Eliminate distractions.** Turn off your cell phone. Close your office door. Try an app that will lock down your internet access beyond your immediate task. The biggest trick of social media is making you feel indebted to it, especially if you use it for business. But guess what? You won't have a business if you're spending time that should be used researching, accounting, planning or resting for scrolling.

4. **Learn to do things now.** For two weeks, focus on attacking any work that needs to be done immediately. It doesn't matter if it's preparing a report at work or having a talk with your preteen at home. *If it needs to be done, do it.* View it as an experiment. If you're unhappy with the results, you can return to your old ways.

5. **Be thorough when completing tasks.** It's not enough to get things done. *A good work ethic also consists of doing quality work.*

   - It's easy to fall into the trap of getting things done quickly and just "good enough," but poor quality work will often come back to haunt you.

A solid work ethic creates powerful results. We know someone with minimal skills who is successful. This is because they likely have a solid work ethic. Imagine combining a solid work ethic with your intelligence, education, and other skills.

A Guide to Planning Your Week

Most of us attack the week one day at a time. We get to the office on Monday, get a cup of coffee, and then allow our emails and spontaneity to dictate the flow of that day.

Consider how things could work out better if you have a weekly plan for your life before you wake up on Monday morning. And don't just plan your work-related items; plan everything else too. Figure out what needs to be done and prioritize those items.

For your best results, avoid living life as it unfolds. ***Taking control will increase your confidence, help you stay ahead of your work, and help you find more free time to do whatever you like.*** So, give it a month and see if you enjoy the benefits.

Follow these steps to create
a plan for the week:

1. **Have a weekly planning session.** Sunday is the logical choice. You've decompressed from the previous week, but it's still fresh in your mind. The workweek starts in just one day.

    - Your items will vary with your individual life. Whether using a post-it note or a Google Docs file, almost everyone has a system for creating and editing their "to-do" list. Too often, though, these lists are just an assortment of ideas and tasks that need to be completed in the future and not-so-distant future.

    - Make a list of tasks for each area of your life. The areas might include work, personal items, and family.

    - An example: WORK
        - complete marketing project with LaTeefha
        - interview applicants for the medical assistant position
        - contact the vaccine management company to discuss inventory issues
        - find a contractor to change the ballasts in the nurse's station

2. **Assign priorities to all of the tasks.** *Assume that you can't get it all done.* Which items must be done, and which can slide until the following week?

   - Assign one of three levels of priority to each task. For example, you might use 1, 2, 3, or A, B, C, or Red, Yellow, or Green.

   - Start with your number 1 priorities and complete them before moving on to the number 2 and 3 priorities.

3. **Schedule these tasks into your calendar.** Begin this process by Sunday evening. Then, you should know how you will spend your Monday morning. Don't wait until your alarm clock wakes you up.

   - There is nothing wrong with maintaining a to-do list, as it can make the difference between getting stuff done and going crazy trying to keep everything organized in your head. Still, the typical to-do list leaves much to be desired.

   - Unlike a conventional to-do list, having a prioritized schedule furthers your planning, allowing you to increase efficiency and productivity. A prioritized schedule puts things into perspective, allowing you to figure out what truly needs to get done at this moment and focus on that.

   - Avoid over-scheduling. Once you fall behind, it becomes impossible to catch up. Leave room for emergencies and requests from the boss. *Schedule 50% of your time and leave the rest available.*

Using Delegation to Balance Your Life

If you're like many people today, you've got all kinds of things going on in your life: work, school, kids, household duties, and countless other things that can wear you out and bring you down. The good news is *you can avoid feeling stressed out and out of balance* by delegating some of what you do to others.

Doing it all isn't necessary! Instead, ensure that you take time for yourself and get the people around you to shoulder their share of the burden. There's nothing wrong with working hard and trying to do all you can for your family, but they should also give back to you. Love from them is great, but how about some help with the dishes and laundry, too?

Know When to Delegate Chores and Tasks

Whether there are chores around the house or tasks at work, you can hand some off to other people, so the workload is distributed more evenly. There's no shame in that, and it's not the same thing as having someone else do all the work while you sit back and do nothing. Instead, you simply understand that *one person should never be expected to do it all.*

If you and your spouse work full time, for example, a system where only one of you does all the household chores is one-sided and can lead to resentment. It puts your life out of balance and can make you angry and irritable. It's much better to sit down and *come to an agreement on who will perform which chores and then stick to it.*

If you have children, they can also take part in chores. Even if they're young, teach them to put their toys away and keep their rooms neat. Then, as they get older, give them more responsibility until the household "runs itself" more efficiently.

Work should be delegated in similar ways throughout an office environment. The best leaders are not the ones who can complete the most tasks but the ones who can teach others to understand the need to master those tasks, then motivate them to take ownership of them. If you duplicate yourself, it frees you up to add value elsewhere in the organization.

What Does Delegation Give You?

The delegation of chores and tasks can bring balance back to your life. If you're seeking that balance, understand that you can find it right now through delegation. It's worth it. You're worth it! Having balance in your life is essential for both physical and emotional health, and you cannot achieve balance if you spend all your time doing things for others.

Some of the things you do must be done for you. Take a walk, get some exercise, play a game, or simply sit quietly and read a book or watch a movie. Maybe you just want some extra sleep. No matter what you desire; it's time to get it back and bring your life into balance. Start today, and move forward.

In no time, you'll see that you feel better physically, and your emotional state and outlook on life are both more positive because you have balance. Just as physical balance is necessary to keep a person walking straight and moving forward, emotional and life balance are needed to stay on the right path toward overcoming problems and finding more joy in everyday things.

Resist Media Multitasking

Multitasking feels good in the short term. Crossing multiple items off your to-do list is stimulating and satisfying. However, you may still need some support to help change your habits.

Try these strategies to break the
media chains that bind you:

1. **Understand how your brain works.** Media multitasking is problematic because you're doing complex tasks that draw on the same resources. For example, it's best to avoid talking with your child about their day and responding to texts simultaneously because both require your full attention.

2. **Shut off your phone.** Remove the temptation to check your messages—power off your phone, tablet, and other devices for a few hours a day.

3. **Post your hours.** Maybe you're concerned that others expect you to be accessible throughout the day. Let them know when they can reach you and when you'll be offline.

4. **Schedule breaks.** You're more likely to multitask when you're losing interest in something.

Take a 10-minute breather each hour to
avoid the temptation to multitask.

5. **Do a status check.** Catch yourself when researching medical symptoms and editing a marketing proposal simultaneously. Slow down. Switch to doing one thing at a time.

6. **Alternate between activities.** You can still juggle multiple responsibilities and pastimes. Arrange your workday so that you update your software or clean up your inbox in between calling clients. If you've been cleaning the garage all morning, take a walk before you tackle the basement.

7. **Think long-term.** You'll avoid multitasking when you keep the long-term consequences in mind. Imagine how much you'll enjoy thinking more clearly and having increased energy.

The Two Most Effective Ways to Increase Your Productivity

Increasing productivity means increasing earning potential.

If you own a business providing any service, improving your ability to deliver the service in less time will allow you to take on more clients and earn more money.

Likewise, if you sell a product, finding a way to make or deliver that product faster will enable you to serve more customers and make more money.

You're more efficient when you find ways to do the same thing in less time. So efficiency and productivity go hand in hand.

The more efficient you can make the process of completing any task, the more productive you'll be.

Use these strategies to increase your efficiency and be more productive:

1. **Seek out and accept specialized help.** Whether you run your own business or are a stay-at-home mom or dad, it will save you lots of time and energy at the start if you're open to collaborating with others.

- Mark Zuckerberg may be quite capable of developing all the new programs needed to advance Meta while working with prospective clients and handling customer service and PR. However, Mr. Zuckerberg and most other successful individuals would never be caught doing this.

No matter how much you can do by yourself, your resources are limited by one factor that trumps all others - TIME.

- So, rather than spend 8 hours a day answering phone calls, working on new products, shopping for groceries, and cutting your own grass it may be a more productive use of your time to zero in on the one or two things that give you the most results for the amount of energy that you put into them.

- For example, if developing a new product or course will eventually double the size of your business by being able to cater to an additional market or consumer demographic, then this is time well spent.

Paying someone else to answer phones and freeing up your time to be devoted to projects that will give you more returns for your time invested is the sign of a true boss. Combining this strategy with a prioritized schedule will enable you to focus on what's most important for you and get it done. Trust me, your productivity will soar!

The End.